Going On

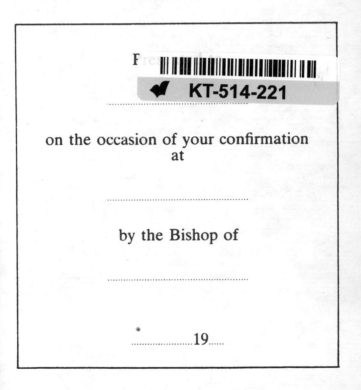

Presented to

....

on the occasion of your confirmation
at

....

by the Bishop of

....

................19......

Going On

Guidelines for the Newly Confirmed

JOHN B. TAYLOR
Bishop of St Albans

DARTON · LONGMAN + TODD

First published in 1989 by
Darton, Longman and Todd Ltd (Daybreak imprint)
1 Spencer Court
140–142 Wandsworth High Street
London SW18 4JJ

Reprinted 1991 by Darton, Longman and Todd Ltd
(Daybreak imprint)
Reprinted 1993 and 1994 by Darton, Longman and Todd Ltd

British Library Cataloguing in Publication Data

Taylor, John B. (John Bernard), *1929–*
   Going on.
   1. Christian church. Confirmation
   I. Title
   265´.2

ISBN 0–232–51859–9

The Scripture quotations in this publication are from the Revised
Standard Version of the Bible, copyrighted 1971 and 1952 by the
Division of Christian Education of the National Council of the
Churches of Christ in the USA.

Phototypeset by Intype, London
Printed and bound in Great Britain by
BPC Wheatons Ltd, Exeter

Contents

Introduction

Since I became a bishop in 1980 I have confirmed anything between five hundred and a thousand candidates every year, many of them adults. Those who are in their teens seem to have developed the habit of receiving presents as well: Bibles, prayer books (usually the Alternative Service Book), manuals about the Holy Communion and other Christian handbooks. It is a good trend, but I wonder how well they are used. Perhaps my conscience is accusing me because I was given a little book when I was confirmed in St Mary's Watford in 1945, and I confess that I never got round to reading it. It was too stodgy by half.

This little guidebook for the newly confirmed has few merits, I suspect, but I have tried very hard to make it readable. After all, what is the point of writing what few people will read? It is addressed mainly to young people and I hope that if any older confirmees find themselves reading it they will not dismiss it as being too light-hearted. But I have geared it to those who are young in the faith and who are looking for guidance about going on in the Christian life. I try to take nothing for granted, even at the expense of appearing to oversimplify.

It is of course written with members of the Church of England in mind. But I should like to think that young Christians of any tradition would find it helpful if they found themselves reading it by accident. After all, its theme is all about growing in Christ and most of us need help in that direction.

Finally, I am grateful to the publishers for inviting me to 'put down in writing some of my confirmation addresses to see if they would make a book'. I have not done what they asked because that would have cleared me out of sermons, but instead I offered a selection of talks for the newly confirmed which I have always wanted to give but never been able to. It is dedicated to all those whom I have confirmed and all those who are yet to come, with my gratitude for the privilege of being allowed to lay my hands upon them.

April 1989   JOHN ST ALBANS

Your Confirmation

Being confirmed is a big moment in anyone's life. It only happens once. It comes after weeks if not months of preparation. It involves major decisions. Like marriage it entails the taking of life-long vows. It is not something to be undertaken lightly.

That does not mean that you can't enjoy it. You should; and if your family and friends, your grandparents and godparents can get along as well, it makes it a family celebration for everyone. It is after all a very special day. Remember the date. It can go down in your diary along with your birthday as one of the great and memorable days of your life.

Why is it so important? Let me give you three reasons. First, because it is *an answer to prayer*. It may not have dawned on you that might be the case, but think for a moment. When you were very small all kinds of people, many of whom you will never know, showered you with love and kindness, and some at least will have expressed this by praying for you. Your parents would have prayed for you – before you were born, as soon as you were born and constantly ever since then – or if they didn't, some

1

godfearing relative or friend of the family would have done so.

I think of the day when my twin daughters were born early one Friday morning in St Helier Hospital, Carshalton. As soon as I received the phone call that at last they were on the way, I dashed up to the hospital on my bicycle, with my legs feeling like jelly, and was dressed up by the nurse in apron and face-mask to be allowed into the labour ward to see what my wife had produced. It was an ecstatic moment, but the very first thing we did was to pray together for those gorgeous babies and to ask God that they would grow up to give their lives to him and love and serve him. Now, your father may not have been a young curate like me when you were born, but I am quite sure both he and your mother have said many silent prayers for you in the course of your life. Even atheists and agnostics pray, when they really care, though they rarely admit the fact. So you can see your confirmation, your public statement of your Christian belief, as the long-awaited answer to someone's loving prayers.

Secondly, because it is *a big decision* for you. You probably thought a good deal about it before ever you signed up for the confirmation preparation class but during the preparation too you thought carefully about whether you wanted to go through with it and if you were ready to make this life-committing decision. It may not have been all that easy to say yes. On the other hand you may have been longing to make public the decision you took in your heart of hearts ages ago, that you wanted to be known as a follower of the Lord Jesus Christ and a committed member of his Church. But to go public as a Christian is a big step and one which you will, I hope, never regret.

Thirdly, your confirmation is an important day because it represents *a new start*. It is like the opening of a door which leads in to communicant membership of Christ's Church. From now on you are no longer a junior member but a full member, able to take full advantage of your privileges and to draw more deeply on the resources that are offered you in the service of Holy Communion through the Body and Blood of Christ. I shall be writing about that later on, but because it is such an important part of following Jesus it makes the moment of confirmation a very special event – the beginning of a privileged life.

There is another question that I must touch on before we go any further, and that is 'What exactly *is* Confirmation?'. To put it another way: Who is doing the confirming?

You could well answer that *the bishop* is doing the confirming, and that would be perfectly correct. The confirmation card or certificate that is given out will probably give the name of the bishop you were confirmed by. You may even have his signature to prove it. By the way, do remember the name of the bishop who confirms you and when you meet him again go up to him and say, 'Hello, Bishop, you confirmed me.' Bishops love to meet those whom they confirmed and even though they can never remember the thousands that pass through their hands, they like to be reminded that some at least of their confirmation candidates have not forgotten it but are grateful for what it meant to them and for the person who performed the ceremony. With any luck you might even be able to tell the bishop what he preached about or what his text was, and that will make his day.

Yes, the bishop does the confirming. He does so because he is a leader in the Church and he represents the Church worldwide. It is an excellent tradition of the Church that although all clergy may baptize, only bishops may confirm. By so doing he is reminding you in effect that your membership is not just of the local church and that you become a communicant member of St Mary's but that you are being received into communion with all with whom the bishop is in communion in the wider Church of God. You become part of a worldwide fellowship and will be recognized as such in any part of the Anglican Communion.

The bishop does this by praying for you and laying his hands on your head. This is very personal and it makes it special for you. We read in church history of occasions when a visiting bishop on horseback might have arrived in a certain place and conducted a mass confirmation of all those who had been waiting since his previous visit several years before. They could hardly have enjoyed a personal laying on of hands, which is what the service demands. Apart from anything else, the imposition of the bishop's hands has symbolic meaning. It signifies the touch of God upon your life and his interest in you personally. It is something to feel and to remember.

Alternatively, you could answer by saying that *you* are doing the confirming, and that too would be perfectly correct. The origin of confirmation is that it is the rite of personal commitment when the candidate takes upon him or herself the promises made for them by the godparents at their baptism. This of course only applies in the case of infant baptism, for those who come to confirmation unbaptized have the great benefit of being conscious of their baptism, which probably takes place at the confirmation service itself and is conducted by the bishop just before the laying on of hands.

But whether you are confirming what someone else once said on your behalf or are making the promises for the first time, the declarations you make are sweeping and very committing.

The first is '*I turn to Christ*'. The word 'turn' is a gentle word. It does not suggest a heroic act of will, a great decision needing large doses of moral courage. Nor does it draw attention to the person who says it, as would have been the case with 'I choose Christ' or 'I decide for Christ'. That would be a trifle too self-centred. The word 'turn' reminds you of turning to face the warm sun or turning your head to see someone better. You are being attracted to Christ, so you turn to look at him. It also means turning round and away from yourself and your sins, as the other questions suggest. It is in fact the simplest word to describe 'being converted', which is also a word meaning 'being turned round'. It is a good Old Testament word too and you find it in phrases such as 'Turn to me and be saved, all the ends of the earth' (Isaiah 45:22). Our Lord used it more than once, as in Matthew 18:3. 'Truly, I say to you, unless you turn and become like children, you will never enter the kingdom of heaven.' So this is what you are doing when you turn to Christ – to face him, to put your trust in him, to look to him as the one direction of your life.

Then comes *'I repent of my sins'*. You could well argue that this ought to have come first because the correct order is repentance and then faith. But I imagine those who constructed the service were thinking that it is only in the light of Christ that a person is impelled to repent of their sins. But the fact remains that the very first thing we need to do as we look to Jesus Christ is to turn away from the sins that have kept us from him.

To repent is much more than being sorry for our sins. Of course we are sorry for everything about us that defiles us in God's eyes and contradicts his holiness. We will come increasingly to see our sins as the cause of Christ's death on the cross, for they all contribute to the burden of the world's sins that he bore for us there. And if that does not make us feel ashamed and want to hide our face, I don't know what will. But to repent of our sins means not only to be sorry but to change our minds. Instead of being enticed and attracted by sin (and it can be devilishly attractive), we turn our backs on it. We ask forgiveness for all the sins we have committed (most of which we have forgotten or are scarcely conscious that we have committed) and we resolve with God's help not to do them again. That is repentance, and it is coupled with the faith that looks to God to help us in this resolve.

Thirdly, we say *'I renounce evil'*. Whereas repentance is the way of dealing with the past, now we are looking to the future as we turn to Christ and live our lives in him. Once again the great alternative, the enemy of our Christian faith, is sin. In personal terms he is the devil, or Satan (the Hebrew word for 'the adversary'), and the old Prayer Book called upon us to 'renounce the devil and all his works'.

If your father was a hereditary peer, which I imagine is highly unlikely, and you were the eldest son, then on his death you would automatically inherit his peerage. From being just 'The Honourable' you would become 'Lord So-and-So' and you could then take your seat in the House of Lords and enjoy all the privileges of the upper class, including being bombarded with begging letters! If you did not relish this prospect or had a rooted objection to being in the aristocracy, the only way you could avoid it is by a legal process involving renouncing your title. It has to be done once and for all. You could not go back on it and later change your mind. It is an act of renunciation.

So with renouncing evil. It is a solemn saying no to the devil and everything he stands for. Once and for all.

All this is your part, confirming the promises which were made in your name by your godparents. The act of confirmation is something you do, and the rest of the congregation listens to you doing it and bears silent witness to these sweeping words of commitment.

However, to get back to the question of who is doing the confirming, it would also be possible, and perfectly correct, to say that *God* is confirming you. The wording of the service actually says so. 'Confirm, O Lord, your servant . . . with your Holy Spirit,' prays the bishop as he puts his hands on your head.

We are here moving out of the realm of confirming promises to confirming people, a very different thing. In the case of promises, to confirm means to ratify, to reaffirm; in the case of people the word means to strengthen, to make firm. This is precisely what we ask God to do – to strengthen you by his Holy Spirit. How does he do it?

Well, for a start he strengthens you in your Christian faith by the simple act of your declaring your trust in Jesus publicly. Doing this in church is relatively easy because you are surrounded by friendly, praying people. It is much harder to admit that you have turned to Christ in front of people who think that is silly, but you have to learn how to do it and you will need to be pretty brave to do so and not mind a few sniggers. St Paul in his letter to the Christians in Rome reminds us that 'if you confess with your lips that Jesus is Lord and believe in your heart that God raised him from the dead, you will be saved. For man believes with his heart and so is justified, and he confesses with his lips and so is saved' (Romans 10:9f). So public confession of your faith is a great source of strength.

God also strengthens you through the prayers of the congregation. They are there in church to support you in prayer and no doubt they will continue to do so as you grow in the Christian life. It is a great thing to know that you are being prayed for. When I was much younger an elderly clergyman said to me, 'John, I'm going to pray for you. When's your birthday?' I said, 'May the sixth. Why?' 'Right,' he said, 'I'll pray for you every month on the sixth of the month.' And so he did, and wrote to me on my birthday every year until he died. Often I would remember that it was the sixth of the month and say to myself, 'I'm being prayed for today.' It was a great encouragement to me.

And then there is the laying on of hands. The bishop's hands are a sign of God's fatherly hand being upon you. They touch your head and you experience the sensation of the physical contact. It speaks to you of God's contact with you. He is saying: I know who you are, I love you, I want you, I promise you my help, just as you have promised me your life.

The confirmation service sometimes ends with the prayer:

Heavenly Father, we pray for your servants upon whom we have now laid our hands, after the example of the apostles, to assure them by this sign of your favour towards them.

May your fatherly hand ever be over them, your

Holy Spirit ever be with them. Strengthen them continually with the Body and Blood of your Son, and so lead them in the knowledge and obedience of your word, that in the end they may obtain everlasting life; through Jesus Christ our Lord, Amen.

Whatever you may feel about it, you should find yourself strengthened, confirmed in your faith by God as a result of confirmation.

So there are three aspects of the service: the bishop confirms you, you confirm your promises and the Lord confirms you by his Spirit. There is a lot going on in your confirmation and it is all for your benefit.

Follow Me

One day Jesus was walking by the Sea of Galilee and he saw Simon and his brother Andrew casting a net into the sea in the hope of catching some fish. He called out to them, 'Follow me and I will make you become fishers of men.' The story in St Mark's Gospel simply adds: 'And immediately they left their nets and followed him.' Now obviously there was much more going on than those few words suggest, and we would love to know more. Was this their first encounter with Jesus? Surely not. What happened to their nets, their boats and all their equipment? Who took them over? And how immediate is immediately? It sounds a bit unreal as it stands in the New Testament.

But it is certainly not unreal to talk about following Jesus and his call to people like us to follow him.

Someone has said that the whole of Jesus' teaching can be summed up in three phrases: Come to me; follow me; abide in me. To sinners who need forgiveness he says 'Come to me'. Come and begin the Christian life. Come and receive the forgiveness of your sins. Don't stay away any longer. 'Come to me, all who labour and are heavy laden, and I will give you rest. Take my yoke upon you, and learn from me; for I am gentle and lowly in heart, and you will find rest for your souls' (Matthew 11:28f).

To those who come to Jesus, he says something else: 'Follow me.' As if to say, you came for what you could get and needed, but now I am asking you to come with me wherever I go and to be not just a Christian but a whole-hearted Christian, a disciple, walking in my footsteps and doing as I say.

That was how he gathered his followers around him, and they stayed together for the best part of three years. But then on the last night he spent with them on earth he asked them to do something else: 'Abide in me.' Stay close, even though I am going away and you are not going to see me again. I shall be there with you but I shall be invisible. I want you to live as closely to me as a branch is part of a tree, drawing upon its life and bearing its blossom and eventually its fruit. That's how close I mean; and I shall be even closer to you.

Three short phrases. We thought about coming to Jesus in the previous chapter when we tried to explain what it meant to turn to Christ. And most of this book is going to be about abiding in Christ and how in practical terms you keep in touch with him and stay close. So that leaves the middle phrase, 'Follow me', to talk about now.

It does not mean giving up your job or leaving school straightaway and becoming a missionary, even though it *appears* as if that is what Simon and Andrew actually did. But I cannot believe that Our Lord's call to us to follow him means that we all leave our daily occupations and take up other work that is 'more Christian'. It is only a very few people that Jesus calls to special, full-time service; most of us he expects to get on with our daily living *as followers of his*.

The fishermen left all and followed. And everyone who wants to be a follower of Jesus has to leave things behind. Things that get in the way, things that take up undue time and attention, things that are given false importance and detract from our discipleship. There are undoubtedly some things that have to be abandoned, and we shall realize gradually what those things have to be. But first let us list the positive aspects of what it meant for Simon and Andrew to follow Jesus Christ.

1.   From that moment on *Jesus became the centre of their lives*. They were increasingly caught up with him and his divine calling. Their lives grew more and more intertwined with his and they became more and more dependent upon him. It was a two-way process really because they were also part of his support group, so the benefits were mutual. But having once begun to follow him not one of the twelve was tempted to go back and leave him in the lurch. At any rate, not until the very end.

Some deserted him. When his words were particularly hard and uncompromising there were usually some who slipped away unobserved and followed him no longer. But they were not the inner circle of the twelve, just general followers – who fluctuated between fascination and curiosity, part of the inevitable crowd that always gathers round a controversial figure. They liked to see miracles, they loved his confrontations with the Pharisees, they were impressed by so much that he said, but they were all the time suspicious of him. He was not quite the sort of Messiah they were looking for.

But for the twelve disciples he was everything. He allowed them to share some at least of his thinking. They were still not too sure who he was – a prophet certainly, but was there anything more? It seemed so, but you could never be sure. However, there was no doubting his magnetism, the attractiveness of his utterly holy life and his loving character. The fact was that you could not spend long with him without being affected by it, and that meant being changed for the better. He had that effect upon you – and he still does.

The difference between the sun and the earth is that one goes round the other. We used to think that the sun went round the earth, a typically man-centred way of looking at things (though thoroughly understandable). Now we know that the earth goes round the sun and we have to be much more respectful towards it. Similarly, people who respond to the call to follow Jesus have to switch from being self-centred beings for whom he is a distant, controlled object in space, to going into orbit around him because we discover that he is the one central point in the universe around whom we all revolve. It is the gravitational pull of his personality that changes us, and we willingly become his planets, his satellites.

2. *Jesus Christ became their constant companion.*

14

They always say that you have to live with someone in order really to get to know them. And I have heard it said that many a preacher's reputation for sanctity has been dependent on the silence of his wife. Certainly it is very difficult to pull the wool over the eyes of those who live with you day in and day out. They see you as you really are.

For the disciples to live alongside Jesus was no disillusionment. He was genuine, transparently so. He was quite uncannily free from sin. They saw him on parade before a crowd and they saw him in his unguarded moments. They saw him tired and depressed, they saw him angry and upset and they saw him elated. They saw how he behaved with women. They noted his attitude to money and possessions. And what they saw in him they were to imitate in the years after his death and resurrection.

This was what it meant to them to follow Christ. Not everyone wanted to do it. He himself had discouraged some by saying 'Foxes have holes and birds of the air have nests, but the Son of man has nowhere to lay his head'. It was like that, literally, more often than not. But his continual presence made it worthwhile.

There were times when he was not around: when he was away on a hillside praying or had let them go on ahead while he was caught up with his own concerns. Then things often went wrong. That was the time when they began bickering at each other or arguing over their seniority in the Kingdom he was going to establish. They seemed to have a gift for letting him down as soon as his back was turned.

When he was there, however, things were so different. And most of the time he was.

For today's followers too Jesus is to be the constant companion. Better still, he never goes away from us or turns his back. 'Behold, I am with you always to the close of the age' was how he put it in his last words to his followers. Now that he is no longer limited by time and space, he can be alongside us and within us every moment of every day. And it is living in that awareness that describes what it means to follow him.

3. *His task becomes their task*. Hitherto it had been fishing and family life that absorbed their attention. Running a small business cannot but give you a one-track mind, if you are going to be successful; and the small businessman is always dreaming of success. Until they were called to follow Jesus, Simon and Andrew had come across him down by the river Jordan, when John the Baptist was preaching and baptizing, and had been caught up in the enthusiasm of believing that here at last was the promised Messiah (John 1:40–42 tells the story). But the discovery had not made any material difference to their daily life, except perhaps to prepare them for the day when Jesus would find them at their nets by the Sea of Galilee and summon them to leave all that behind. Certainly their ready response to the call is more understandable in the light of what St John tells us about an earlier encounter.

Now I hope I have made it clear that following Jesus does not mean that every follower gives up their livelihood and leaves the family home. But it does mean a change of priorities, so that our absorbing interest becomes doing God's will and material goals tend to take second place. I was brought up on the story of the man who, when asked what his job was, said, 'My job is to tell people about the Lord Jesus Christ, and I pack pork to defray expenses.' I realize now that that man (probably mythical anyway) had a pretty poor theology of work, but at least he was absorbed in God's work, as the Galilean fishermen came to be.

'Follow me and I will make you become fishers of men.' Our Lord's calling was to seek and to save the lost, to bring men and women out of their darkness of unbelief or ignorance or superstition into the light of the gospel. He came to call sinners to repentance, to open the eyes of the blind, to proclaim liberty to captives. He used so many images to describe his task in life, but all of them related to a ministry to people and bringing them to God.

That is the Christian follower's absorbing interest too. In a very small way he is to be a mini-evangelist, a fisher of men (and women), a person who identifies with Jesus' ministry to those who are lost or in need.

A survey was conducted recently among a number of Christians of different ages and backgrounds and among the questions asked was how they had come to their Christian faith. In the vast majority of cases it was due to the influence of one person, usually not a preacher or a minister, but a friend. So bringing people to Christ is not a highly specialized task. It can be done by anyone who has come to him and knows the way. And if you have said yes to the

Lord's call to you to follow him, then you will find yourselves sharing his vision, joining in on his work and winning your friends to Christ.

4. *They became learners.* The word disciple means just that, learners. From the moment the two fishermen joined the group of apostles they became learners. Jesus was the travelling rabbi, or teacher, and they were his band of pupils.

Much of Jesus' teaching was done in front of a crowd. The Sermon on the Mount is the obvious example. But there were other occasions when he took his disciples aside and taught them privately. He taught them how to get at the meaning of parables. He taught them about prayer, including the Lord's Prayer. He gave them a lot of help about 'the last days', the events attaching themselves to the end of the age. And we still read and benefit from that teaching to this day, though often we find it difficult to understand and only wish we could have been there to have asked supplementaries.

There is no doubt about it, Jesus was a marvellous teacher. You can study his technique and see how gifted he was. The parable-story was a brilliant way of conveying an important idea through a memorable medium. Many of his sayings were in poetical form with a balance and brevity that made them stay for ever in the hearer's mind. His words were punchy, crisp and catchy, and the weightiest ones were driven home with a 'Truly, truly, I say to you'.

To be in the company of such a man was an unforgettable experience and though the Gospels give the impression that the disciples did not learn a great deal during their time with the Master (they kept on making fools of themselves), it is clear from the Acts of the Apostles that after the resurrection they found themselves calling to mind his teaching and putting it into practice. It was as if all they had learnt from Jesus built up like the wood of a huge bonfire, and it needed first the realization that he had risen from the dead and then the gift of the Holy Spirit at Pentecost to set light to it and make it ablaze with light and fire.

Today's followers too are like people who enrol in Christ's school. There is so much to learn, so little time in which to learn it, but you have an admirable teacher to learn from. It will demand effort on your part – no learning comes easily – but that is precisely what the Lord is calling you to do, when he says 'Come, follow me'.

5.   *They were prepared to take risks.* Obviously it was an enormous risk to abandon your boat and your nets and to go after a little-known prophet, but it was the kind of risk-all faith that the Lord frequently called for. He had little sympathy for the man who wanted to hang on to his security at all costs.

One of Jesus' hardest sayings is found in Luke 14:26, where he said, 'If anyone comes to me and does not hate his own father and mother and wife and children and brothers and sisters, yes, and even his own life, he cannot be my disciple.' This sounds appalling teaching from the founder of a religion that has always advocated the blessings of family life and personal responsibility. It is of course very starkly put, but I am quite sure that what Jesus was saying was that you could not be a disciple if you held on to any priority, however legitimate, over and above your obedience to him and your commitment to following him. This understanding of the text is made more obvious when you realize that in Hebrew the words 'to love' and 'to hate' are not as black and white as we think of them, but mean 'to put first' and 'to give second place to'.

Jesus wants followers who will give him pride of place and will take risks in company with him. You remember his rather scathing parable about the man who buried his talent and did not even bank it in order to make some profit on it for his lord's sake. In the same sort of way, he expects us to risk everything for him and to live dangerously, or to put it in more biblical language, 'to live by faith'. That is the kind of life to which he calls us and which we accept if we follow him. It's a tall order.

Do This in Remembrance

'Do this in remembrance of me.' Jesus' solemn words spoken at the Last Supper in the upper room on the night of his betrayal are repeated at every service of Holy Communion, the Eucharist or the Breaking of Bread. The service has many names and many meanings and because Christians regard it as so important they get very attached to the particular meaning which they themselves hold dear. As a result the service of Holy Communion has, tragedy of tragedies, been a focus of division and argument among Christians of differing traditions. It was intended to be a focus of unity.

Nevertheless it is a very precious occasion and you will never get on particularly well in the Christian life until you have learnt how to make the most of what it has to offer. This takes a long time so don't expect to make progress too quickly. But it is worth persisting, indeed you must persist, because doing this in remembrance of him is the Lord Jesus' strict instruction to his followers and we ignore it at our peril. He instituted the service for our good and we are foolish if we do not derive the benefits which he intended us to have.

As I have already said, different traditions give the Sacrament of Holy Communion different emphases and you will have been taught by your own priest or minister how to approach it in the way your church celebrates it. I do not want to cut across that. Instead I want to give you some help which may enable you to grow in your appreciation of this great sacrament and to value it increasingly over the years.

I associate this service with four ideas and I want to say something about each of them. They are remembrance, communion, feeding and proclamation.

First, *remembrance*. This is at the heart of the service. I am quite sure that Our Lord's command to do this in remembrance of him was made because he knew that without it there would be every temptation to forget or to distort what he had done. But as it is we re-read reverently the narrative of the Last Supper with Jesus' words of institution, and we are recalled to think carefully about his death and resurrection. So a good deal of thinking is involved.

We remember the Lord Jesus at supper with the twelve, who then became the eleven as Judas left them and went out into the night. We feel the tension between the prospect of what lay ahead the following day and the Lord's desire to treasure these last moments with his friends. We remember the pathos of talk about betrayal coupled with the unspoken fears in the hearts of the disciples as they thought they knew what was going on but did not dare put it into words in case they were correct. We remember those symbolic actions with the bread and the cup and the new meaning in which they were being clothed.

And then our memories move on to the day following, Good Friday, and we relive in imagination the sufferings of our Saviour on the cross. We stand momentarily with his mother Mary and the apostle John at the foot of the cross and remember the look on his face as he put into words his loving care for them: 'Woman, behold your son' and to John, 'Behold, your mother.' Our thoughts move on to the resurrection on Easter Day, with the discovery of the empty tomb, the appearances of the risen Christ, the ecstasy of the disciples as it dawned on them that he was really alive and had conquered death.

All this, and much more also, is what we remember. Though we can of course remember it any day of the week and in any place, we have this priceless opportunity to do so on the Lord's day, in the Lord's house and in the company of the Lord's people. There is no better setting for our remembrance and without this facility, provided by the service of Holy Communion, we shall all too easily forget. You can understand therefore why it is that you are urged to be regular at this service and not to neglect it. The Lord knows that you need to be there – to remember him.

The second word is *communion*. Sometimes it is called fellowship, or sharing. It reminds us that the Sacrament is not just a private act of devotion. It is a means of linking Christians together with each

other and with their Lord. So there is nothing wrong
with being conscious of our fellow-worshippers.
Sometimes we use the Peace in the middle of the
service to greet them. This is not a belated 'good
morning' which we may have forgotten to do at the
church door. It is a conscious reminder that we are
brothers and sisters, united in Christ, and about to
be joined to each other and to him in a common
meal. So the barriers have to come down and sometimes hatchets have to be buried as well and quarrels
patched up.

Our communion is also expressed in saying the
prayers and the Creed together, and in some churches the whole congregation stands with the cel-
ebrant through the whole of the great Eucharistic
Prayer as a sign that we are all priests together
uniting in celebrating the sacrament of our redemp-
tion through Christ. There are numerous opportunities in the service for our private thoughts and
devotions, but communion is essentially a corporate
activity and we learn to enjoy doing it together.

It follows from this that we should not attend
Communion and then completely ignore our fellow-
worshippers after the service or during the week. By
being together at the Lord's Table a bond exists
between us which should make a difference to our
relationships. We could well start off by getting to
know a few people's names, and going out of our
way to be friendly.

Then comes *feeding*. The actual receiving of the
bread and wine is to my mind the heart of the service. For to me it is not ordinary bread and wine. I

receive it as the Body and Blood of Christ, and as I put it in my mouth I say that I am feeding on Christ in my heart by faith with thanksgiving.

I am not going to enter into the argument about whether the bread and wine actually change their character in the course of the service, for that is a theological minefield and differing Christian traditions hold strong and often irreconcilable views on the subject. What I am concerned about is not so much what happens to the bread and wine, but what happens to you when you eat and drink it.

The invitation to come forward to receive the sacrament often uses words like these: 'Draw near with faith. Receive the body of our Lord Jesus Christ which he gave for you and his blood which he shed for you. Eat and drink in remembrance that he died for you and feed on him in your hearts by faith with thanksgiving.' They are marvellous words and they contain so many of the right ingredients for feeding on Christ to the benefit of your own soul.

Draw near: you have to get up out of your seat and come forward. As you come you will probably echo the words of that lovely hymn,

> Just as I am, without one plea
> But that thy blood was shed for me,
> And that thou bid'st me come to thee,
> O Lamb of God, I come.

Faith: which makes you say, I believe in Jesus. I trust him, I turn to him, I rely on him. Without his grace I shall go away hungry and helpless.

Receive: I hold out empty hands, because I have

nothing to give. All I can do is receive from the one who is the great giver, who gave himself for my sins and the sins of the whole world.

His body, his blood: the Lord who at the Last Supper said 'This is my body, this is my blood' is now making the self-same offer to you. A body that was broken for you on the cross, just as that piece of bread was torn apart as a visible reminder of what he went through, and the life-blood that trickled down his face and ebbed out of his veins as he died for you. Receive it, take it into yourself, make it yours, feed on it and draw strength from it.

With thanksgiving: as you go back to your place and kneel quietly there you will find yourself saying over and over again, 'Thank you, Jesus.' Thank you for loving me, thank you for dying for me, thank you for giving yourself to me. Thank you, Jesus.

With thoughts like these you will find yourself feeding on Christ in your heart, and the service of Holy Communion will never be dull or meaningless. If it is, it will be entirely your own fault. The important thing to remember is that the Lord is there, if only you will come to him, receive him and feed on him.

The last word is *proclamation*. When Paul wrote to the Corinthians about the Eucharist he said: 'For as often as you eat this bread and drink this cup, you proclaim the Lord's death until he comes' (1 Corinthians 11:26). What he means is that the service of Holy Communion is an enacted sermon. It proclaims to the world the gospel of the dying and rising Son of God. It can have a powerful effect upon those who attend it, even if they have not yet become Christians. It was one of the great evangelical leaders of the Church of England, Charles Simeon, who dates his conversion, his spiritual awakening, to the time when as an undergraduate he attended Holy Communion on Easter Day in King's College Chapel, Cambridge.

At a much more modest level I remember talking with a man in his thirties who was wanting to offer for the ministry and I asked him my usual question about how he came to faith. I was given a long answer about how he and his wife had moved down to Portsmouth, and though they were not church-goers the combination of being in a new home and the coming of Christmas made them feel they would like to go to the nearby church. He told me, 'I didn't understand much of the service, but it was a Communion and most of the congregation went forward to the front. My wife and I stayed in our places because we knew it wasn't for us. But I couldn't help noticing the woman sitting in front of us. When she came back to her place after receiving the bread and wine I could tell from her face that something had happened to her. It was real, and I thought I must find out what it was. So I did.'

Any church service, but a Communion service particularly, has a great converting power. It is proclaiming the Lord's death, and we are to go on proclaiming it until he returns to this earth at his Second Coming. Then eucharists will be no more, for they will be replaced by what the New Testament calls 'the great marriage-feast of the Lamb'. Then we shall see him face to face and not through a glass darkly. Then we shall not need bread and wine; we shall not need reminders. For the great fulfilment will have come. Christ will have returned in glory.

Finally, let me give you a few practical hints to help you to get the most out of the Holy Communion, for a lot of people miss out on what it could mean to them.

1. Come to it in the right frame of mind. Look forward to it and expect to get something out of it. Many Christians spend a lot of time preparing themselves for it, especially those who only receive the Sacrament occasionally, say once a quarter. Don't let it ever be treated casually. After all, you are coming to meet the Lord and to receive him into your life.

2. Do some self-examination. Roman Catholics take this particularly seriously and will often go to confession before attending Mass. We should learn from them to be much more disciplined about our sins and our relationships with other people. The Prayer Book issues this invitation to those who come to Communion: 'Ye that do truly and earnestly repent you of your sins, and are in love and charity with your neighbours, and intend to lead a new life, following the commandments of God, and walking from henceforth in his holy ways; draw near with faith and take this holy sacrament to your comfort.'

It is enough to stop you in your tracks for a moment and make you think twice whether you are fit to come to the Communion of Christ's Body and

Blood. Your fitness is not a matter of how good you are but how repentant you are, and whether you are taking your sins seriously. Sadly we do not use those old words as often as we might, and we can easily sidestep the necessary preliminary stage of examining ourselves before we come to receive the Sacrament.

3. Use the silences. There are usually quite a number of these, when the priest is preparing the Lord's Table or while you are waiting for others to receive. You can, if you want to, just sit and stare but you will be missing a good opportunity to remember. So use those silences to remember the Lord Jesus and to think about his great love in dying on the cross for you. Imagine him hanging there and open your heart to him in wonder and gratitude. Use the words of hymns which you can memorize to express your thoughts in prayer. Hymns such as 'When I survey the wondrous cross', or 'It is a thing most wonderful' or 'There is a green hill far away'.

The best time of all is after you have received the bread and wine and have returned to your seat. Don't just sit back; think about what you have done. You have eaten the Body of Christ and drunk his Blood. You are feeding on him. You are receiving him by faith. So echo the words of the child's prayer:

> Into my heart, into my heart,
> Come into my heart, Lord Jesus.
> Come in today, come in to stay,
> Come into my heart, Lord Jesus.

Then you will find yourself saying with real meaning:

29

'We thank you for feeding us with the body and blood of your Son Jesus Christ. Through him we offer you our souls and bodies to be a living sacrifice. Send us out in the power of your Spirit to live and work to your praise and glory.'

Growing Up

'We are to grow up in every way into him who is the head, into Christ' (Ephesians 4:15). There is not much point in being born unless you are going to grow. Babies are weighed regularly to see how they are developing and proud parents often keep a record-book of when the first tooth appears and when the last nappy is discarded. At least, they do for their firstborn; after that the novelty wears off.

Being committed to Jesus Christ is like a new beginning, a new birth. The Christian is someone who has been born again. Don't let that title be commandeered by a certain type of American Christian who uses the term to distance himself from others. Every person who has turned to Christ and received him into their lives can be described as born again. Be proud to be among the number of the twice-born!

And now you are to grow. Too many Christians suffer from arrested development. They regard their confirmation as a kind of passing-out parade, an end rather than a beginning. They remain 'babes in Christ', stunted in a permanent infancy. Make sure that doesn't happen to you.

31

The way to grow is through a generous use of what are called 'the means of grace'. Grace is a difficult word because it has so many meanings. You say Grace before meals and the Grace at the end of meetings (and those are two totally different meanings and sets of words too), and it is a quality of courtesy and kindliness. But the New Testament word 'grace' means God's favour shown to those who do not deserve it. To that extent we rely every day on God's grace. It is God's grace that saves us, helps us, strengthens us, encourages us and forgives us. We cannot survive without God's grace. The very fact that we are Christians is by virtue of his grace. 'By grace you have been saved through faith; and this is not your own doing, it is the gift of God' (Ephesians 2:8). We may have produced the faith, but then we soon discover that it was God's grace that enabled us to do even that. There is no virtue attached to believing in Jesus. Our faith was drawn out from us by his loving kindness. As the hymn-writer put it:

> For every virtue we possess
> And every victory won,
> And every thought of holiness
> Are His alone.

There are a number of standard means, or channels, through which we receive God's grace. There are plenty of non-standard means as well but I want to say something about the regular ways we can draw upon God's help.

The first is quite clearly the Eucharist, and the

chapter on 'Remembering' has dealt with that, so I need not add anything more – except to underline the fact that this is not an option but a direct command from the one who knows best. 'Do this in remembrance of me.' Our motives in going to Holy Communion may be mixed, partly out of obedience, partly out of habit, partly out of a desire to meet with Christ and draw strength from him. Motives will always be an odd mixture. The important thing is that we should be there. The rest will follow.

The second means of grace is prayer and we shall be saying more about that in the chapter on 'Keeping in touch'. At first sight it may seem unusual to think of prayer as a means of grace, unless we mean grace for other people, i.e. the people we pray for. But prayer is much more than asking God for things. It can have very considerable benefits for the person who does the praying as well. For the essence of prayer is being in contact with God, sometimes without a word being spoken.

This was how Jesus spent long hours in prayer with his heavenly Father. He was alone with his thoughts in the conscious presence of God. He poured out his heart to God, he thought about the decisions he was going to have to make, he wrestled with questions about his own identity and vocation, he interceded for his friends and the people he was ministering to, he would have yearned in love and longing for the world he had come to save. At the end of his time of prayer, however, he was strengthened. He faced the temptations and demands of the new day with greater freedom and confidence. He had been renewed by being in his Father's presence.

If this was the case with Jesus, how much more will it be for us? If he needed to pray, how much more do we need to?

Thirdly, I mention the Bible, though that too is so important that I shall speak about it later on under the heading 'About books'. It is the Christian's guidebook, prayerbook and textbook all rolled into one. It is the Word of God, inspired by the Spirit and given to us to reveal God's will and purpose for his creation. It teaches us the way of salvation. It points us to Jesus and brings us closer to him than any other means at our disposal. It is a vast reservoir of spiritual wisdom. We cannot do without it and little growth is possible without a regular diet of what it contains. The apostle Peter told his readers to 'desire the sincere milk of the word that you may grow thereby', so clearly we shall need to give a good deal of attention to the part the Bible and daily reading of it has to play in our lives.

Next comes the fellowship of a worshipping congregation. I am often asked if it is possible to be a Christian without going to church, and my answer is always the same. Of course it's possible, but you will grow up as deprived as the child who has never lived in a family. The fact is that you need others around you and they need you. It is of course much more than going to church that you need to do, it is being part of a church that you need to be. You need a pastor to care for you, older Christians to be an example to you and to encourage you, friends to be helped by and a Christian family life to grow up within. It is the God-given way of keeping your faith alive. Take a glowing coal from out of a fireplace and put it to one side and it will quickly lose its redness and turn to a dull grey. It retains its glow only by being with others who are also aglow with the love of God. The same is true of you, and of every Christian.

This is much more than occasionally attending a service. It means being a full, voting, worshipping, active member of a congregation. To start with it may not be easy for you to be accepted. The usual complaint is that 'no one ever speaks to me'. To which the answer is 'Well, go and speak to them.' Don't be put off by the slow progress you make. Use the time to demonstrate that you are going to be a loyal and regular member of your church. Join a home-group if you can find the time. Offer to do some work for the church, not up front but in a menial capacity. My first church work was to sweep the confetti from the church porch after weddings on Saturday afternoon so that it was looking nice for the services on Sunday. The trouble was that not many people saw me doing it! But it was a start. Handing out the hymnbooks was one of the more advanced echelons of Christian service, suitable only for the favoured few.

Christian service is also a means of grace. Obviously in any organization there are jobs that need doing and they have to be shared around, but the important thing about Christian service is that it gives you a sense of responsibility. A small area of

God's work is dependent upon you for its success. It may not be precisely what you would like to do or feel most fitted for, but that is secondary. If in doubt go up to your minister and tell him that you would like to do something for God and you are at his disposal. Once he has recovered from the shock he will take your offer seriously and suggest something. Then, for goodness sake, do it. If you make a mess of it he may switch you to something else, but don't immediately turn your nose up at the first job you are invited to do. Remember, it is a means of grace and of growth.

So far I have mentioned only a range of what might be called 'spiritual exercises'. But one of the finest means of grace is not something you do but something you face, namely, adversity. This comes in a variety of forms. Probably at its worst is outright persecution, of the kind suffered by Christians in countries where Christianity is an outlawed religion. England used to be like that, during the persecutions of some of the Roman emperors, and I have a particular attachment to the first English martyr, St Alban, who was put to death for his faith as early as AD 209. And as the remains of the city where he lived, Verulamium, are just down the hill from where I live, and the place where he was martyred now has my cathedral built over it, he becomes a very important figure in my thinking. The simple fact of history is that whenever persecutions have hit the Church, faith has invariably been strengthened and the Church has come out of it healthier and more vigorous than before.

The persecutions you and I have to face are much more modest but that does not mean to say they are not painful. A young person finds ridicule particularly difficult to bear and no one likes to feel elbowed out of the company he wants to be in because they take against his Christian witness. So these are the fiery darts which we have to face, some malicious, some thoughtless, but all hurtful. And yet to rise above them is the finest test-bed for Christian character that I know.

There is another side to adversity which comes not from people but from circumstances. There are some days when everything seems to go wrong and you wonder what you have done to deserve it. I can think of a teenage girl who gave her life to Christ and was brimming over with the joy of her new-found faith. But within a fortnight she found her boyfriend had jilted her, her mother had been taken ill with a suspected cancer and her exam results were not good enough to get her to the university she had set her heart on. 'Is this what Christianity does for you?' she wailed as she told me about it. I told her that this was not the first time a young Christian had been subjected to this kind of attack. 'I get the distinct impression', I told her, 'that someone somewhere wants to wreck your Christian faith. The devil doesn't like people becoming Christians, so it's not surprising that he counter-attacks.' This sort of thing happens too often, to my mind, to be a coincidence, but the Lord knows and will see you through if you keep on trusting him. Easy words, but hard to live by. And yet there is nothing quite like adversity to bring out the courage, the determination and the faith which will win through and bring you out on the victory side.

Probably the hardest battle we have to fight is the battle against depression. Some people are more prone to it than others, and I am not referring to really serious clinical depression which needs expert psychiatric help. I am thinking of those awful feelings of flatness or darkness which come upon you, when your emotions go dead, your Christian faith seems empty and you feel out of sorts with yourself and the whole world. Sometimes you can identify the reason for it: a relationship that has turned sour, a disappointment, guilt over something that has gone drastically wrong or, in some cases, you have been working too hard or under extreme pressure and this is how it has hit back at you.

Under such circumstances all you can do is hold on. It helps to keep on going through the motions of your Christian life, saying your prayers, reading your Bible, going to church, even when it appears to do you no good at all and you feel an absolute hypocrite to be doing it. After all, isn't your conscience telling you that the best thing you can do is jettison your Christianity and not act a part any more? If it does, don't believe it. It's just the depression doing what depressions always say and do – telling you what a failure you are. God never says that to you: it is always the voice of the enemy. God's Spirit is called the Comforter, which can equally well mean the Encourager, and he is there to build you up not to rub your nose in the dirt.

But why, you may ask, does he do nothing to ease your feelings of depression? Quite simply, because there are times when you must necessarily *feel* alone and those are the very times when you can learn to live by faith and not by feelings. Your feelings are an unreliable guide to your experience of God. You believe God and trust in him whether he feels near you or miles away from you. When feelings recede, as in times of depression, faith can come to the fore.

It has certainly been my experience that the low times have been the times for spiritual advance. They have provided the chance to learn lessons about God which can be learnt in no other way. It is a form of adversity which I would rather be without, but when it comes (and you will not avoid it) it can produce valuable results.

As you will see, there are many means of grace provided by God so that you may grow up into Christ in every way. The time will come when out of your own experience you will be adding your own suggestions to the standard list of means of grace. Let me add one of my own: music. Paul in his letters to the Ephesians (5:19) and the Colossians (3:16) makes much of psalms and hymns and spiritual songs. They are the accompaniments of the spiritual life and can be wonderfully enriching. Musical tastes vary from person to person. One may adore negro spirituals while another goes over the moon about Duruflé, and someone else wants to chant repetitive choruses. The height of the brow doesn't matter! The key thing is that the music, and especially the blend of scriptural words and evocative music, draws

39

you closer to God and lifts your worship to a higher plane.

If you are fortunate enough to have a musical ear, or better still if you have some musical talent with an instrument, you are well set up to develop this particular means of grace. What is more, you can use your gifts to bring blessing to other people.

Remember always what the goal is: that you may grow. It is a process that will never end this side of glory. It leads you onwards and upwards and its purpose is to prepare you for the day when you will see him face to face. It may seem a very long way off, but make sure you are going on that path and you make use of all the means at your disposal.

Keeping in Touch

'Lord, teach us to pray', said one of Jesus' disciples, 'as John taught his disciples' (Luke 11:1). He was answered with the Lord's Prayer, the parable of the importunate friend and some memorable gems about answered prayer. But what interests me about the story is that the followers both of Jesus and of John the Baptist thought that prayer was something they needed to learn about and be taught.

The same is true today. A series of addresses on prayer will always command a good audience, and for my part I have never sat through a talk on prayer without learning something that has helped me. Prayer is, almost by definition, something we know we ought to be better at and would be glad of help with. So this chapter is going to be about prayer and I am going to divide up what I want to say under a set of questions: what, why, when, where and how?

What is prayer? The simple answer is to say that prayer is talking with God. Not a monologue, but a conversation. A conversation implies meeting and spending time together in each other's company. It means that some of the time you are speaking and some of the time you are listening. It also means that some of the time no words pass between you at all. You are just enjoying each other's company. And if you are engaged in doing something together, words will be few because you are both intent on the job in hand.

All these are factors in prayer, and straightaway they rule out some of our misconceptions, e.g. about prayer being a long list of intercessions, or that you cannot pray when you are busy doing something, or even that prayer is a one-person occupation. We forget that God is involved in prayer quite as much as we are.

But why pray? Because God wants you to. That should be sufficient reason but I had better fill it out. God wants you to pray because this is the way he has ordained that human beings should keep in touch with him. He has not asked for rites and incantations. He does not want us to dance like dervishes or howl and beat gongs to attract his attention. He wants us to go into our room, shut the door and pray to our Father who is in secret. There is no other way.

God also wants us to pray because he is our heavenly Father who loves us. Any parent whose children are away from home will tell you how they long for the telephone to ring and to have one of them on the line for a chat. It makes their day. So is it not entirely reasonable that the God who has created and redeemed us loves to hear from us and to be in touch with us?

A further reason why we pray is because we need to. If prayer was no optional extra for the Lord

Jesus, it is even more of a necessity for us. He drew great strength and courage from the nights he spent in prayer, and it would be very foolish to suggest that we could do with less. If anything we should be spending more time in prayer than Jesus did, but the only point I really want to make is that prayer must play some part in our lives because it played such a large part in his.

Then again, other people need our prayers. Prayer is like a network of support which criss-crosses the world and joins people together in a greater harmony and fellowship. It guarantees that you do not feel isolated. It brings comfort and strength through the sheer knowledge that others are praying for you and showing their love and concern in this costly and time-consuming way. And if you have ever been prayed for a great deal, as I have been (for people are very kind in praying regularly for their bishop), you will know that to be borne up on the prayers of others is like being in a hovercraft carried along over the waves on a cushion of prayer. I have found it to be quite an uncanny experience, tremendously uplifting, and I only hope that those whom I pray for have the same story to tell of being supported in a wonderful way by the prayers of those who care about them.

Finally, the reason we should pray is so that we can get to know the will of God. Let me put it like this. The more you pray the more sensitive you become to God. So, for instance, you soon discover that you cannot pray for revenge on someone who has done you a wrong. The words will stick in your throat, because your conscience tells you that such a prayer is not God's will. In more delicate areas of prayer too you will find that part of the exercise of prayer is discovering what it is that God wants us to pray for. So we do not go barging into God's presence telling him all our wants and desires, we try out our prayers on him to see how we should express them in accordance with his will.

This is the kind of exploratory prayer that you find frequently in the pages of the Bible. As for instance when Abraham was interceding for Sodom and was sounding God out to discover if he would spare the city from judgement if there were fifty righteous people in it – or twenty? Or ten? (See Genesis 18 for the full story.) Or again, was the God he was learning to obey the sort who demanded child sacrifice, as most of the other gods of the Near East appeared to do in Abraham's day? The story of the sacrifice of Isaac in Genesis 22 gives God's clear 'no' to that particular exploration, showing how the firstborn had to be redeemed with an animal sacrifice but nothing else.

You will find that you learn to pray by praying, and you get to know God's will as you grow in the practice of prayer. That alone is sufficient answer to the question 'why pray?'.

Where and when to pray? Anywhere and any time are suitable for prayer. There is no place where you can't and no time that prayer is inappropriate. You can pray sitting in an armchair or lying in bed. You can pray on a bus or on a bicycle (eyes open, of course!). But you will want to find a suitable place and time when you can have a set time of prayer and this needs careful management. For although prayer can be done anywhere, the daily appointment with God in prayer should never be crowded out, except for a very special reason.

In order to find this time, and it needs to be quality time, you will have to work on your daily timetable (if you have one). The start of the day is best because there are fewer interruptions and you can control your time with the help of an alarm-clock. If the early morning is one frantic rush, all you need to do is get up ten minutes earlier and have some time alone with God before the frantic rush begins. Some people prefer the evening or mid-day. I occasionally see businessmen reading their Bible in the train on the way to work and I imagine that when their eyes close they are quietly praying and not just nodding off.

The set time of prayer, which is often called the Quiet Time, is no substitute for other brief moments of prayer, nor are they any substitute for the Quiet Time. A pause to say Grace before a meal is a useful reminder of God's presence and your gratitude for the gifts he gives you day by day. A brief offering up of the day to God as you go to bed combined with a prayer for forgiveness for the things you got wrong, makes a suitable finale to the day. Or if your prayers are reserved for the evening, do at least greet your Lord as you wake up and consciously give your life and the new day to him.

How to pray?

(a) Daily. Just as regular meals are important for

health, so regular prayer should be part of your daily routine. It's quite as necessary as cleaning your teeth! The one thing you must not do is pray when you feel like it. Apart from the fact that you may not feel like praying all that often, the time when prayer is most needed is when you feel least like doing it. So to develop regular habits of prayer can help to tide you over those difficult patches. Don't worry if you miss a day for some reason: you oversleep or the day's programme goes all haywire. Just apologize to God for missing your appointment and make sure you fit it in the following day.

(b) Briefly. God is not impressed with long prayers but on the other hand he deserves more than a fleeting conversation or a shouted greeting. 'Never mind the length, feel the quality' is what you should go on. Some of the most effective prayers in the Bible are very brief. They are sometimes called 'arrow-prayers' because they are short and carefully targeted, like blind Bartimaeus crying out 'Jesus, son of David, have mercy on me!' or Nehemiah offering a quick prayer to God when he was in conversation with the King of Persia (Nehemiah 2:4). Set times of prayer can be more leisurely than that, but they do not have to be wordy or interminable. It is best to begin with a fairly brief Quiet Time and only lengthen it as you find you want to spend longer and do more with the time at your disposal. So five minutes will very soon extend to ten minutes and it will not be long before you find a quarter of an hour is cutting it rather fine. But start small.

(c) Quietly. Someone has said that the only two

ingredients of a good Quiet Time are quiet and time.
Certainly quietness is important, and it is not easy
to come by. A noisy household, a shared bedroom,
incessant music do not make for peaceful oases for
prayer. Maybe you will have to concentrate doubly
hard or plan to have your prayer time when the
noises have died down. Some people find they can
pray while they take a walk, but they then have to
find another time for reading the Bible.

(d) Sincerely. It should go without saying that
God expects us to be sincere, but what I am asking
for is total honesty in our praying. We must watch
that we do not dress up our prayers into what we
think is acceptable language when we are really
deceiving ourselves and pulling the wool over God's
eyes as well. There are times when we have to tell
God frankly how we feel – hurt, let down, angry,
miserable, complaining. We shall not stay like that
for long because the very act of praying in those
terms will turn out to be a healing process and we
shall see our problems or complaints in a better
light, but it is far better to say what we think and
let God straighten us out than to be mealy-mouthed
about ourselves in order to ingratiate ourselves with
him. The Psalmist said, 'Behold, thou desirest truth
in the inward being; therefore teach me wisdom in
my secret heart.' And his continuing prayer in Psalm
51:6–12 is a masterpiece of honest talk which we
would do well to imitate.

What to include? Prayer has a variety of moods
and we must beware of getting stuck in a rut. We
need to try them all so that our praying is well-

balanced and complete. Five themes come quickly to mind: worship or the adoration of God, confession of our sins, intercession for other people's needs, thanksgiving for God's blessings, and finally dedication of ourselves to him. You can also add prayer for your own personal needs but I hardly think you will forget to include them.

Worship comes naturally at the beginning, though it can recur at other stages throughout our prayers. The start of prayer has to do with getting in the right frame of mind and coming into the conscious presence of the God who is always there. This is helped by the reading of an appropriate verse or passage from the Bible (Isaiah 40, Psalm 95, Revelation 4 or 22 are particularly helpful chapters) or a worshipful hymn. Always have your Bible and a favourite hymnbook near you when you say your prayers. Then with your eyes focused on the Lord you can praise him and express your worship and adoration of him. Be quite unashamed to say that you love him, either in your own words or using someone else's, e.g.

> Father, we adore you;
> Lay our lives before you;
> How we love you.

The second and third verses simply change the word 'Father' to 'Jesus' and 'Spirit', so it is not particularly profound. But its simplicity and the tune that goes with it are quite captivating.

Quite soon your worship will lead you into confession of your sins, for the contrast between God's

·wonder and holiness and your selfishness and petti-
ness is very marked. It is not sufficient just to grovel
and to say what a wretch you are. The Lord knows
that already and I doubt if you will sound very con-
vincing anyway. No, confession is for specific sins
on which the Holy Spirit puts his finger and for the
sinfulness which mars and disfigures even the good
things that you try to do. Repentance does not mean
sweeping all our failings under a carpet of generaliz-
ations about our own unworthiness. It means taking
them out one by one, looking straight at them, giving
them their correct names and then throwing them
out of the window in an act of rejection.

Now that is highly colourful language to convey
what I am trying to say. The point is that you cannot
repent of your sins unless you know what they are
and are prepared to do something about them. Only
that kind of confession and repentance leads on to
forgiveness and absolution.

At this stage it may be helpful sometimes to use
one of the confessions found in a prayer book, if
only because they are followed by an absolution
which it would be valuable to read as the conclusion
of this section. At the very least remind yourself of
God's promise of cleansing and forgiveness,
enshrined in a text such as

If we confess our sins he is faithful and just and
will forgive our sins and cleanse us from all
unrighteousness. (1 John 1:9)

or

49

'I am he who blots out your transgressions for my
own sake and I will not remember your sins.'
(Isaiah 43:25)

The knowledge that your sins are forgiven through
Christ gives you a light-heartedness and freedom to
bring your various petitions to God. So you readily
move on to intercession. We teach children to pray
with the help of the fingers on their hands. Each
finger stands for someone to pray for, especially if
first you tell them to put their hands together in an
attitude of prayer. The thumb is the smallest of the
five and is nearest to you, so you pray for yourself,
your family and all those who live nearby. Your
index finger points the way and reminds you to pray
for leaders, teachers and clergy who guide you in
the right path. The middle finger is the tallest and
so you pray for rulers and for all those in authority
in the world. The fourth finger is the weakest one,
so you remember the poor, the sick and those who
have no one to pray for them and care for them.
The little finger is furthest away from you, sc you
pray for missionaries and all those who are far from
home.

That's not a bad way to begin. Of course, you will
get more sophisticated as you get further into prayer
and the time will come when you will develop your
own prayer-list of people you want to pray for daily
or weekly or even on a monthly cycle. This will
need to be kept carefully up to date, be occasionally
pruned and often added to.

Just recently I visited the home of a retired

missionary couple. In their one-roomed flat they had a large sheet of plasterboard on the wall covered with a great collage of photographs of their friends from all over the world. Many of them were fellow-missionaries but of course the pictures showed a good many of the African Christians they had once worked among. It was their visual prayer book, and every day they sat in front of it and remembered before God each one of the people whose photographs were there on the wall. It not only rekindled their memory but it helped them to pray imaginatively and regularly for God's blessing on their brothers and sisters in the Lord.

Thanksgiving can come anywhere, because it should percolate all our praying and probably will without much difficulty. I find it a good starter to prepare the way for worship, but in any event it comes as a marvellous antidote to feeling sorry for yourself. 'Count your blessings, name them one by one, and it will surprise you what the Lord has done.' When Paul wrote to the church in Colossae he kept emphasizing the need for thankfulness in the life of the believer and ended up by saying:

> And whatever you do in word or deed, do everything in the name of the Lord Jesus, giving thanks to God the Father through him. (Colossians 3:17; see also 1:3,12; 2:7; 3:15,16)

Finally, dedication. Every day's prayer needs to conclude with a dedication to God's service. This is our daily act of obedience and submission to God's will. We cannot pray 'Thy will be done' without offering to contribute to the answer to that prayer. God may not want to use us. We may not yet be particularly suitable for his service. But we make ourselves available to him and we ask him to shape our lives so that we can be ready for service when the time comes. And this leads me to my favourite prayer of dedication.

> Lord Jesus, Master Carpenter of Nazareth,
> Who on the Cross with wood and nails hast
>   wrought man's full salvation,
> Wield well thy tools in this thy workshop,
> That we who come to thee rough-hewn
> May by thy hand be fashioned to a truer
>   beauty. Amen.

I hope I have not given the impression that prayer is easy. It is not. Or that it is straightforward. I wish it were. Actually it raises the most profound questions which the greatest minds have not yet solved. And yet, even small children can pray and God hears them. So don't be discouraged or confused by all the complications. Higher mathematics is pretty baffling but I still go ahead and learn to add up.

And don't expect 'answers to prayer', as if God is going to leap into action at the snap of your fingers. Answers will come, sometimes quite astoundingly and not always quite what you asked for, but situations will change and good things will happen as a result of your prayers and that will encourage you. But you will do best at prayer if you learn the important lesson that prayer is not so much a means of changing God's mind but a way in which God can change and shape you. That is what makes it such a valuable exercise. So, get praying.

About Books

Far and away the world's best-selling book is the Bible. It has been published in hundreds of different languages and it is treasured in every corner of the globe. In Britain publishers compete with each other to produce yet another modern translation and each new edition seems to be a financial success. There is a never-ending appetite for the Bible even in the post-Christian western world. And in parts of the third world copies of portions of Scripture are like gold dust, so greatly are they in demand.

Yet the Bible is not one book but a library of sixty-six books, written by many authors in three different languages over a period of well over a thousand years. If it did not claim to be inspired by God, you would have to believe it was in order to explain its astonishing character. For despite the vast time-span between its earliest and latest parts, it has nevertheless been possible to find such a unity of thought running through its pages that scholars can write books on the Bible's theology of man or of salvation or of work or of sex. No other sacred book has such a universal appeal or engenders so much hostility from some and so much veneration from others. It is not a book you can be neutral about, unless of course you never open it.

The Christian finds the Bible irresistible. He finds an instinctive fellow-feeling with it, for he sees his faith mirrored in its pages while at the same time he fuels his faith from its teaching. He discovers that the same Holy Spirit who inspired the authors and has breathed life into the text is the Spirit of Jesus who has brought the living Lord to life within his own heart and mind. He does not have to be persuaded to read the Bible, he turns to it as instinctively as a baby turns to its mother's milk.

The Bible speaks with the voice of authority, the authority of God. Partly because it contains a good deal of 'Thus saith the Lord', but mainly because it carries conviction as being the word of God. And this despite the fact that much of it is narrative or poetry or not very digestible legal material. Its authority derives from God but is affirmed by Christ. For he read the Scriptures (the Hebrew Old Testament as far as he was concerned) as if they were the very words of God, unalterable and authoritative, definitive in argument and to be believed and obeyed. In the light of his attitude to the Old Testament, the New Testament is not difficult to accept in similar terms.

The authority which Jesus gave the Bible and which the Church has consistently recognized is regularly reinforced by the book's converting power. The list of those who have been converted to Christ by reading the Scriptures is endless. It would be easier to compile a list of those who have been converted apart from the Bible!

So this book will have a necessary and important place in your Christian growth. You will read it in your Quiet Time, meditate on it and you will probably want to commit certain parts of it to memory. But first you must make sure you have a nice, readable copy of the Bible which is a pleasure to handle.

Which Version? Well, you will have to choose which you prefer. Here are the most widely used versions available today:

The Authorized Version (or King James's version) of 1611

The Revised Standard Version, published in America in 1952

The New English Bible, a completely fresh translation from the original texts in contemporary language (1962)

The Jerusalem Bible, the work of a team of Roman Catholic scholars (1966)

Today's English Version, the Bible Society's translation into popular English

The New International Version, an update based on the RSV

My personal choice is the RSV or NIV but you must make up your own mind, and all of them are equally good. But do make sure you like the print and the layout and the 'feel' of the book. It makes reading it so much easier.

Where to begin? Not at Genesis or you may never get to the end. You have to be selective, moving from the New Testament to the Old and back again. After all, you wouldn't plough your way through a library beginning with the oldest book on the shelves. The best thing to do is to follow a scheme of daily reading, with notes supplied by the Bible Reading Fellowship, Warwick House, 25 Buckingham Palace Road, London SW1W 0PP or the Scripture Union, 130 City Road, London EC1V 2NJ. Both organizations have graded series of notes for different age – and interest – groups, so you would be sure to find what you wanted from them.

Always read the Bible prayerfully. You are wanting to listen to God and learn from him. There are other times when you will just want to discover what it is all about and then a quick, almost cursory, reading may be suitable. But devotional reading of the Bible on a daily basis is an exercise in drawing near to God and finding in it your spiritual food.

The passage you read will not be long, say, a dozen verses or at most a chapter. Read it through once to get the meaning, and then go back to the beginning and meditate on it a verse, or a few verses, at a time. As you meditate, try to imagine that you are there at the scene of what was going on at the time or that you are one of the early Christians who were listening to this letter of Paul or Peter. Think yourself back into the situation. Then ask yourself some questions.

What light does this verse throw upon God or upon Jesus Christ his Son? Is it saying anything to me about my faith or my behaviour? How do I compare with the example that is being set in this passage? Are there words of warning that I need to heed? Does this passage have any bearing at all on what I shall be doing today? Is there a reminder here of something I may be in danger of forgetting? Can I claim for myself one of God's great promises that are found here?

You have to be very careful that your imagination doesn't run riot and be quite sure that what you are getting out of the Bible is really there and you are not reading it into the text. An elderly clergyman who used to be a great help to me when I was younger said that he looked every day for a WT. When I asked him what that meant, he quoted me Psalm 119:18, the prayer of someone opening the Bible. 'Open my eyes, that I may behold wonderful things out of thy law.'

'You mustn't be greedy, John,' he said. 'Just look for *one* Wonderful Thing each day, and carry it away with you.' So day by day he would read his Bible, find his WT, write it down in a book, think about it frequently during the day and make it his own.

Because prayer is a two-way conversation, and the listening part of it has special meaning for your Bible-reading, it is helpful to turn your meditations into prayer. Share your thoughts with God and resolve before him to put into practice and benefit from the things he has said to you through the passage you have read.

Perhaps it will help if I give you an illustration of what I mean. Let us take a well-known passage from the Gospels, say, John 4:46–54 (RSV). First, read the passage through once.

46   So he came again to Cana in Galilee, where he had made the water wine. And at Capernaum there was an official whose son was ill.

47   When he heard that Jesus had come from Judea to Galilee, he went and begged him to come down and heal his son, for he was at the point of death.

48   Jesus therefore said to him, "Unless you see signs and wonders you will not believe."

49   The official said to him, "Sir, come down before my child dies."

50   Jesus said to him, "Go; your son will live." The man believed the word that Jesus spoke to him and went his way.

51   As he was going down, his servants met him and told him that his son was living.

52   So he asked them the hour when he began to mend, and they said to him, "Yesterday at the seventh hour the fever left him."

53   The father knew that was the hour when Jesus had said to him, "Your son will live"; and he himself believed, and all his household.

54   This was now the second sign that Jesus did when he had come from Judea to Galilee.

Now go back to the beginning and meditate. Like this.

Jesus was back in his home territory of Galilee after his trip to Jerusalem. Back in Cana where he had made such an impression and was getting quite famous. That could be dangerous but it would also provide opportunities for ministering to people who

otherwise might not have heard of him. Publicity
has its good side as well as its bad. Here comes an
official, quite an important person for he had servants, and pleads with him for help. His son was at
the point of death. Interesting. People often only
turn to God for help as a last resort, when all else
has failed, when they are desperate. Not a very
respectful way to treat God, but Jesus is not
offended. Well, not as much as he could have been.

He does, however, fob him off with an exasper-
ated 'Unless you see signs and wonders you will not
believe'. What does that mean? You're only here
for the miracles? Or if there is something in it for
you? We are all a bit like that. Get very keen on
praying and church when we're at our wits' end. I
must remember to turn to Jesus for his own sake
and not for my own. But good for the official: he
stuck at it. 'Sir,' – that's more respectful – 'come
down before my child dies.' He really was desperate,
and it showed. Moral: never be put off by God's
delaying tactics – they are sometimes sent to test out
our seriousness in asking.

Actually, his was a pretty poor prayer, full of
theological mistakes. 'Come down', as if Jesus was
incapable of doing anything for his son without being
personally present. The official had not heard of the
centurion who had simply said 'Lord, say the word
and my servant will be healed'. But perhaps that
hadn't happened yet. 'Before my child dies', as if
Jesus' power to heal was ended once death came.
That wasn't true either. Think of Jairus's daughter,
or the dead son of the widow of Nain, or Lazarus.

But the Lord doesn't correct our theology, shaky as it is; he listens to our deepest needs, however we express them. That's comforting to know.

Then to prove that he could heal from a distance, Jesus says laconically, 'Go: your son will live.' That really was a test of faith. Would I have gone away, or would I have gone on badgering the Lord to get him to come down home with me, just to make sure? What if I got back home and found no change, or worse still, that the child was dead? 'The man believed the word.' That was remarkable. It completely justified Jesus' action both in testing his sincerity and then saying the word of healing. He must have known the man was genuine, and of course – as always – he was right. So I suppose the Lord can tell if I am genuine in some of my prayers too. I must watch that. Beware of signs and wonders for the sake of it.

'He went his way', but he must have wondered all the time. It was a long walk from Cana to Capernaum, more than a day's journey unless you began very early. He stayed the night en route and set off again in the morning. Then he met his servants coming to meet him. His heart sank. Was it bad news? Or could it be good news? Even quite strong faith has its doubts. Good news, and it was written all over their faces. When did it happen? Yesterday, at the very moment when Jesus said the word. Marvellous. Now he really could believe, and he'd get all the family to believe too. Just wait till I tell them.

'This was the second sign.' What of? Long-distance healing? Perhaps. More likely of growing faith. 'Believe' comes three times in the story. I wonder when the official 'believed'. When first he came to beg for Jesus' help? When he was fobbed off and showed he was serious? When he went home because Jesus' word was good enough for him? Or when he discovered the chronological coincidence of the timing? They were all stages in the growth of faith. How many of those stages have I reached yet? I've got a long way to go. I really must learn to trust Jesus with all my needs and to accept what he says. Today.

I'm sorry I have gone on so long but that is the kind of meditation which a passage like this gives rise to. I shall then want to turn my thoughts into a prayer and so round off my Bible-reading before I move on to the other aspects of prayer we were thinking of in the previous chapter. I am not too sure about deciding on a WT. There were quite a few in that passage. Maybe you would like to choose one and begin your own daily collection.

After talking about the Bible it is a bit of a come-down to refer to other kinds of reading matter. But every kind of reading feeds the mind, either for good or ill, and you will want to develop good reading habits so as to give yourself a well-stocked mind for the future. I make no apology for being a great enthusiast for good Christian literature. There are some excellent books in print, thousands of them, and reading a few of them helps to make up for the lack of long and meaty sermons which congregations of an earlier generation used to benefit from (at least I think they did!). Visit a Christian bookshop or sample the church bookstall and you will soon see what a rich and varied diet is available for you at very modest cost. Better still, borrow them from your church library.

Obviously you must follow your own taste and interests. People's stories always make good reading, though I prefer biographies to autobiographies. I suppose I am never quite sure how much of it to believe when the author writes about himself. But beware of getting depressed because you cannot produce as good experiences out of your own past history. As long as you remember that any Christian's achievements are no more than God has allowed him to do, or has done through him, then you will give God the glory and not begin to feel jealous or inferior. I have a marked antipathy to books which are designed to do me good, or to preach at me. (I hope this one is not in that category.)

In due course you will gather your own library of books that have helped you. When you find a really good one, lend it to someone else, because we all benefit from personal recommendation. In my view every Christian needs to have a few basic textbooks to help him to grow in the Christian life. First and foremost comes the Bible, as I have already said. But alongside it you could well do with a Bible Commentary, which explains difficult passages in the text, and/or a Bible Dictionary, which will supply you with a wealth of background information about the Bible and its contents. I have yet to find a better combination of the two than *The Lion Handbook to the Bible*, which has sold well over a million copies and to which (I have to be honest) I contributed two or three pages a very long time ago.

If your Bible does not have a shortened version at the back, a very useful tool is a Concordance. This gives the Bible references for a large number of key words that occur in the Bible, so if you are desperately trying to remember where the parable of the prodigal son is to be found, all you need to do is look up the word 'prodigal' and there you have it – Luke 15. Actually, that's not true because the word 'prodigal' does not come in the Bible: it's a description we have come to give to the parable, but you will find it under 'far (country)' or 'Father, (I have sinned)' or 'elder (son)'. A Concordance is a wonderful invention and when it comes to buying one I suggest you get the largest one you can find or afford.

To this basic collection you will want to add at least one book about prayer, and perhaps one or two books of prayers so that you can draw upon the spirituality of some of the great saints of the past. Anything else must be chosen according to your interest or your felt need at a given time. But remember that God has given you a good mind and he expects you to use it, to feed it and to help it grow in wisdom and the understanding of his will. I promise you, you will never be bored.

This is the Way

Tucked away in the Old Testament you will find this verse: 'Your teacher will not hide himself any more but your eyes shall see your teacher. And your ears will hear a word behind you, saying, "This is the way, walk in it," when you turn to the right or when you turn to the left' (Isaiah 30:20f). The teacher referred to is God and the promise being made to the people of Jerusalem, who are being addressed, is that with God's help they will know the way they are to go.

It is a cheering message and Christians have often taken over the promise of Isaiah and applied it to themselves. They feel confident that in their own lives and in the decisions they have to make they will not be left entirely alone, but that God will give them his guidance. This then is the subject for the present chapter. How can we discover the way God wants us to go?

Life is full of decisions and choices. Sometimes we wish there were not quite so many courses open to us but the choice seems limitless. Choosing a career is terribly baffling these days. There are so many different areas of expertise to choose from, and if you make the wrong decision or if you are made redundant from your chosen occupation, you have to go back to the beginning and re-train so that you can get on to the bottom rung of another ladder. Statisticians tell us that in future most people will follow three different occupations in the course of their working life, in some cases because the occupation will simply die out because of new technology and reduced demand. So the decisions we make at the outset of our career are crucial, and they in turn are governed by everything from the subjects we do at school (where we also have to choose) to the opportunities for training we are lucky enough to get. We can be forgiven for wondering if our lives are at the mercy of some vast, impersonal computer that sorts us out and slots us in wherever the celestial programmer decides. Take heart, it's not quite as bad as that. Many of the decisions are ours and ours alone, and the aptitudes we have and the skills we acquire on the way are our own too. Some things are not in our control, and mistakes will happen for which no one need be blamed, but our life is ours and within limits we can make of it what we will.

There are other decisions too: the way we spend our spare time, the church we join, the jobs we apply for, the place we live, the person we marry, the way we bring up our children. Life is full of major decisions like these and it is quite daunting to think that what we decide on these matters will alter the course of history. Our history, at any rate.

For the Christian, however, there is one major advantage. He believes that God will guide him, that there is a plan for his life which God knows about and that God will not allow him to fritter his life away in a series of wrong and misguided decisions. The Old Testament repeatedly says this. The words 'guide' and 'lead' are two of its favourite verbs. 'The meek he will guide in judgement' says the Psalmist. 'The Lord will guide you continually' (Isaiah 58). 'He leads me beside still waters; he leads me in the path of righteousness' says the Good Shepherd psalm. The New Testament too speaks with the same voice. 'He will guide you into all the truth' says Jesus about the Holy Spirit, and Paul writing to the Romans asks that memorable rhetorical question: 'He who did not spare his own Son but gave him up for us all, will he not also give us all things with him?' (Romans 8:32). Can we really believe that the Lord who has saved us for all eternity will not take an interest in this life of ours on earth and make it of value in his service and a blessing to ourselves and other people? So we come back to the question, how can we discover God's plan for our lives?

The first thing I want to say is that far too many Christians worry about finding guidance when they should be asking God for the courage to make up their minds. Yes, there are pointers to understanding God's will, but in the end you have to make a decision. And it will be based on faith and not on certainty. There will always be elements of the unknown in any decision, and all we can do is by careful thought and prayer to reduce the risks of getting it wrong. But risk there will always be. We live by faith, not by sight.

Having said that, the fundamental criterion of God's guidance for our lives is *the revealed will of God in the Bible*. To say this is to say something positive and something negative. Negatively it is saying that God will never call upon us or direct us to do anything which is contrary to the plain teaching of Scripture. On the positive side is the general statement, for it cannot be more specific, that what God wills for his children generally are the boundary-lines of the path along which we are called to go. That may be depressingly obvious but it has a practical side to it. I have known quite mature Christians who have asked me for help in doing something which they know to be contrary to God's general revealed will but which they would very much like to do and are hoping to get episcopal sanction for doing it. I think of a man who very much needed some money to go to a conference on personal evangelism and who quite unexpectedly found an envelope with five ten-pound notes inside it tucked down the side of an armchair in a dentist's waiting-room, where he was queuing up to be the next victim. He called it a wonderful answer to prayer and was going to pocket it and say nothing about it. He had to be told, gently but firmly, that taking someone else's property is stealing, and it had to be handed in.

Similarly, if the Bible teaches that we are all one in Christ Jesus and that there is neither Jew nor Greek, male nor female, slave nor free, I cannot see how anyone with a Christian conscience can erect barriers of apartheid and claim to be doing it within the will of God. The revealed word of God in the

Bible says it cannot be done. There should be no further argument.

The next criterion I want to put before you is *the path of plain duty*. In many sectors of our lives our choices are limited by the obligations we incur, as members of a family, as citizens of a country, by promises we have entered into, through the responsibilities we hold, by what is reasonably expected of us by other people. It cannot be said too clearly that God's will for us is almost always to follow the path of duty. We may pray for guidance until we are blue in the face but if duty dictates a certain course of action God will be silent. He will not contradict himself to let you do something that is less than honourable.

In the Stock Exchange in the City of London the motto is 'My word is my bond'. In other words you don't need my signature on a piece of paper to prove that I mean it. If I have said it, I'll do it. No argument. There are times when it looks as if the motto is wearing a bit thin, but if a secular community can maintain that degree of honour based solely on the sanctity of a promise it is a remarkable achievement. How much more should members of the Christian community keep their word, however costly and inconvenient it may be. Do you remember the words of Psalm 15 in the old Prayer Book? 'Lord, who shall dwell in thy tabernacle: or who shall rest upon thy holy hill? Even he that leadeth an uncorrupt life: and doeth the thing which is right, and speaketh the truth from his heart . . . He that sweareth unto his neighbour and disappointeth him not: though it were to his own hindrance . . . Whoso doeth these things: shall never fall.'

Then you can be greatly helped by *the advice of friends*, especially those older and wiser than you are. Not all older people are wise, so you will have to choose carefully, because advice is a valuable asset and you want the best available. You are not conducting a Gallup Poll but seeking wisdom to help you in your decisions. The best person is the one who knows you well and preferably has some knowledge of the area in which the decision has to be made. Remember though that no one can give good advice without knowing all the facts, and you owe it to your friends, if they are willing to help, to explain the complete problem and not to keep anything back. Obviously you would only want to do this with two or three people. But when you have sought their advice, and even when asking for it, remember that the decision is yours and not theirs. They can advise, as they see things from their perspective and even as they try to view it from your standpoint too, but you are not to abdicate responsibility from your own decision-making. You have to live with the consequences of the decision and you must have no one to blame but yourself if things go wrong.

Do not ignore *your own personal preferences*. I knew of a young girl who was longing to become a nurse but as she prayed about her choice of career, she felt the one thing she should not do was to be a nurse because it was what she wanted and was therefore selfish and couldn't be God's will. When eventually her minister explained to her that it was quite likely that if God wanted her to be a nurse he would probably have implanted the desire in her heart to become one, her delight knew no bounds. She was freed to do what she wanted to do and what she turned out to be very good at and fulfilled in doing.

What has to be watched is in case your personal preference is built upon greed or selfishness or unworthy ambition. Preferences have to be put through the filter of God's standards of love and unselfishness, but if that is done they can be a pretty reliable means of guidance.

I am never quite sure how much weight should be given to *the combination of circumstances* as a proper guide to understanding the will of God. Some people set great store by circumstances and allow themselves to be led by them in whatever direction they should suggest. Personally I think this is a reflection of their flabbiness and indecision: because they cannot make up their own minds they allow the changing circumstances of life to make the decisions for them. This is what I call the 'celluloid duck' mentality, if that makes any sense to you. The celluloid duck is a lightweight toy you have in the bath with you when you are small, and it bobs around wherever the waves direct it. The Christian who allows his decisions to be made on those lines is really saying 'Inertia rules – OK.'

But sometimes circumstances can be indicative of the right way forward and they are not wholly misleading. The fact is they have to be read and understood, but in the end you make the decisions.

Deciding is the final part of the process. You need to weigh up the evidence that has come from all these quarters and arrive at a decision. Sometimes time is on your side and you can allow the decision to be mulled over. On the other hand, you may have a deadline to work to and it cannot be overstepped. Make your decision, as best you can, in the presence of God. Pray, think, decide, tell God your decision and then go and act upon it, trusting him to see you through.

What if the decision's wrong? Well, it's not the end of the world, and in any case God is pretty adept at making something good out of the second-best – after all, he is doing it continually with people like us! So don't lose too much sleep over the possibility that you might have made a mistake. Most mistakes can be rectified. I once made a decision which at the time I thought was right. It involved a change of job and a move out of my accustomed sphere of work. As I got into the job I began to have an uneasy feeling that I had made a mistake and by the time I had been in it for six months I was almost convinced that this was the biggest mistake of my life. Then things changed. I suppose I was getting used to the work and beginning to master it, perhaps developing a bit of self-confidence too. By the end of the first year I was blissfully happy and I enjoyed every minute of it from then on. It made me cautious about coming to quick conclusions about whether my decisions are right or wrong. Most wrong ones can turn out right, given prayer and persistence.

The one thing I urge you to avoid is putting out fleeces. You may not know about this but it dates back to the days of Gideon in the Old Testament. In Judges 6, Gideon sought the Lord's will in a certain matter by putting a fleece out on the ground overnight, and he asked that in the morning if there was dew on the fleece but the ground was dry this would be a sign that Israel was going to be delivered. Next morning the fleece was sopping wet and the ground was dry. But in order to check that he hadn't got it wrong he asked God the next night that the sign would be reversed, and sure enough the fleece was dry and the ground was soaked with dew.

Based on this story some Christians have developed the habit of setting God puzzles of a similar nature so that they could find out *without any doubt* what God's will for them was to be. Now frankly I think this is impertinent and, while it may have been quite legitimate in Gideon's day – and a bit miraculous too, there is no justification for playing games with God like this in the New Testament era when God has given us his Spirit to inform our thinking and to help us to live by faith. The plain fact is that we can never be absolutely sure: there will always be an element of uncertainty about every path that we tread, and that is part of the adventure of living by faith, as Abraham discovered, when he went out, not knowing where he was to go (Hebrews 11:8). And if we are to live with uncertainty we cannot off-load the responsibility for our actions either by letting others decide, or by letting circumstances dictate our path or by expecting God to show his hand so that we can blame him if things go wrong. Guidance is a matter of being helped to good decisions and trusting God with the consequences.

Eventually the satisfaction of following what we believe to be God's plan for our lives is seen as we look back over the path we have trodden. Whereas, when we look forward, all is misty and unclear, when we look back we can begin to see the pattern emerging and the plan taking shape. We see how God draws into the picture every strand of our lives, mingling them together so that nothing is wasted. We see him making good use even of what we thought to be byways, but somehow he makes sense of them. Most astonishing of all is that he even turns some of our sinful lapses and failures to his glory by weaving them into the pattern and (there is no other word for it) redeeming them so that they can contribute to the whole. Looking back over a long and varied Christian life is a cause for endless satisfaction and thankfulness to God, and the old person who can see the way in which God has led him through life is given special faith and confidence to believe that if he has done that he can also be trusted to lead him safely through the unknown paths beyond the grave. He develops the settled conviction of his security in God which was so well expressed by Paul when he wrote: 'We know that all things work together for good to them that love God, to them that are called according to his purpose' (Romans 8:28, AV).

Testing, Testing

We all know the story of the temptation. 'Then Jesus was led up by the Spirit into the wilderness to be tempted by the devil.' Forty days and forty nights, according to the good old Lenten hymn, he fasted and was tempted in the Judaean desert. If you are not sure of the details, read about it in St Matthew chapter 4.

The story sets the pattern for our thinking. Satan is the tempter and, therefore, we think that temptation is evil and is just a short step away from actually committing sin. We wonder why ever we find ourselves praying in the Lord's Prayer 'Lead us not into temptation'. Would God ever do such a dreadful thing to us?

If you look more closely at the Bible's teaching on temptation you will find there is much more to it than that. If you ask the question 'Who does the tempting and who is being tempted?', you will find that the Bible provides us with four different answers:

  (a) Man tempts man;
  (b) Man tempts God;

(c) God tempts man;
(d) Satan tempts man.

So the position is much more complicated than we might have thought. Let us look at each in turn.

(a) *Man tempts man.* An example of this in the Bible is found in Matthew 22:35. 'A certain lawyer asked him a question, tempting him and saying: "Teacher, which is the great commandment in the law?".' The word used for what the lawyer was doing to Jesus is exactly the same as that used for what happened to him in the wilderness. He was being tempted – by another man. Most modern versions of the Bible change the translation, quite rightly, and say 'testing him'. But it was testing of an unfriendly sort because it is pretty obvious that the lawyer wanted to catch Jesus out and to get him to say something which would destroy his credibility in the eyes of the people. He did not succeed. Jesus outwitted him, as he did to numbers of his enemies who tried him out with similar test-questions throughout his ministry in Palestine.

The Epistle to the Hebrews says that he (Jesus) 'was tempted in all points like as we are, yet without sin'. He did not put a foot wrong.

It is not only lawyers who ask difficult questions, though if you creep into the public gallery of a Crown Court you will hear expert barristers doing their level best to break down an opposition witness by asking searching and sometimes deliberately confusing questions. In biblical language they are tempting/testing the witness, to get at the truth.

But people tempt others in an unkind way. At school you will find children who take great delight in teasing other children about their weak points. They try to make the shy boy blush, they try to make a fragile girl cry or someone who is highly-strung to lose their temper. It is never a Christian thing to do this, but if it happens to you be grateful for it. You are being tested, and, though it may be unpleasant at the time, it can help you to show what you are made of.

(b) *Man tempts God*. In the story of the temptation of Jesus, the devil tempts him to throw himself down from the pinnacle of the temple because God would never let his Son be destroyed and he could be confident that he would be miraculously preserved. And the devil quoted Scripture in support of the temptation. 'He will give his angels charge over you' and 'In their hands they will bear you up lest you strike your foot against a stone'.

Jesus' reply was brief and also scriptural. 'It is written: "You shall not tempt the Lord your God".'

Now I used to believe this was rather a weak reply, as if Jesus was saying 'You mustn't ask me to do things like that. You are not to tempt me.' But what Jesus was really saying was 'I must not tempt the Lord my God'. I must not play games of dare with God and put him to the test by doing stupid things just to see if he will keep his promises. That's impertinent and it is wrong.

God has given us all kinds of promises about protecting and caring for us too. But that is not an invitation to expose ourselves to the enemy's bullets.

We trust in God but we also keep our heads down below the parapets! There are some Christians who take an almost foolhardy delight in seeing how near to the edge of the precipice they can go without actually falling over. That is plain stupid: it is a form of tempting God and we are not to do it. Yes, God *will* care for us and we can look to him for protection and help, but we have to protect ourselves too.

In the Old Testament story of how Moses led the Israelites through the Sinai desert on their way to the Promised Land, they were given all kinds of assurances that God was with them, not least the quite miraculous episode of the crossing of the Red Sea which began the journey. But it was not plain sailing by any means, and the Israelites' disobedience and discontent and downright immoral behaviour tested God's patience and promises to the limit. So, when the apostle Paul looked back on the Exodus story in 1 Corinthians 10:9, he concluded with the words: 'Neither let us tempt God, as some of them also tempted, and were destroyed by serpents.'

(c) *God tempts man*. It sounds a contradiction in terms, but we are beginning to see that temptation is not just a harmful thing, it is a neutral word. It means 'testing', and God most certainly tests us. He does it in order to see what our true calibre is. He does it so that we can learn to draw on the spiritual resources he also provides. He allows us to be put in difficult situations, to suffer hardship, to meet with injustice or pain, because he knows that only by that means can we develop character. God's

78

temptations are not easy, but they are always good. They are given us so that we can be purified, strengthened, refined inwardly.

The parishioner who asked her vicar who called on her one day if he would pray that she might have patience, was dismayed to find him praying that she would have tribulation! 'That's not what I asked for, Vicar,' she interrupted. 'Oh, but it's the way God works,' was the reply. 'Don't you remember what St Paul said? "Tribulation worketh patience, and patience experience, and experience hope." Hardship is the soil in which many Christian virtues grow.'

The lesson came home to me many years ago when I was going through a particularly testing time. Feeling very sorry for myself, I remember opening the newspaper and noticing the text for the day at the top of the personal column. It was the first time I had discovered the verse from Job 23:10. 'He knows the way that I take; when he has tried me [tempted me?], I shall come forth as gold.' It was all I needed to know.

(d) *Satan tempts man*. Here we come to familiar ground. But because we come to it fourth and last, we should be able to see it in better perspective. Satan, or the devil, tests us. The difference between God testing and Satan tempting is purely one of intention. God tests us because he wants us to mature and come through stronger. Satan tempts because he wants to break us and get us down. He does it by trying to crush our spirit under pain or grief; he tries to pervert our natural instincts for selfish ends; he persuades us to become self-satisfied and careless in our nice little selfish world; he leads us into disbelief or distortion about the truths of God. He is not interested in making us better. He only wants to shift us from our hold on God, which is what he tried to do to Jesus in the wilderness.

He is very astute. Not for nothing does the Bible describe him as 'an angel of light'. He quotes Scripture; he gives the impression he is acting in our best interests; he appeals to our vanity; he assures us that this is the way to freedom, to happiness. 'All these things will I give you if you will fall down and worship me.' Or, as the serpent said to Eve, 'Did God say, You shall not eat of any tree of the garden? . . . God knows that when you eat of it your eyes will be opened and you will be like God, knowing good and evil.' The devil's words are very enticing and dangerously attractive. Be warned!

Do I believe in a personal devil? Yes, indeed. If there is a personal Holy Spirit, as the Creeds and the Bible insist, why not a personal spirit of evil? And he can wheedle his way into a human heart and cause untold havoc there. Our Lord told a parable about a person from whose heart the evil spirit had been cast out, but when he was not replaced by a welcome being given to God's good Spirit, he returned 'with seven other spirits more evil than himself, and they enter and dwell there: and the last state of that man becomes worse than the first' (Matthew 12:43–45). With teaching like that, he would be a very foolish person who claimed to believe that there was no such thing as a personal devil. But his disguises are many.

Well then, back to the original question. Why do we pray 'Lead us not into temptation'? Would God ever do that? Yes, he would sometimes, because we could benefit from it. But look again at the Lord's Prayer. We have only quoted half the line:

Lead us not into temptation, but deliver us from evil [or, the evil one].

What this is saying is that if we do find ourselves tempted, we ask to be saved from falling into the hands of the devil. Therefore, the less we are tempted, the happier we shall be! So please spare us from *unnecessary* temptation, because we know how weak and vulnerable we are. And because all too often it is our own stupidity that exposes us to quite unnecessary risks, we ask God that he will save us from ourselves, and spare us from blundering into those moral minefields which can all too easily blow us up.

A final word of encouragement. Temptation is a tough part of the Christian life and we shall often fail. But failure is not the end. God is there to help us up; to forgive us and to wipe the slate clean, and to teach us how to be wiser in the future. So never be ashamed to come back to God again and again to repent and to ask for his forgiveness. He never cuts us off and says his patience is exhausted. He is the eternal forgiver and repairer of damaged lives.

And remember that promise in 1 Corinthians 10:13, 'No temptation has overtaken you that is not common to man. God is faithful, and he will not let you be tempted beyond your strength, but with the temptation will also provide the way of escape, that you may be able to endure it.'

Good Stewards

'As each has received a gift, employ it for one another, as good stewards of God's varied grace' (1 Peter 4:10). That is my text and I want to deal with the subject of stewardship. There are some funny ideas flying about on this word, chiefly that it is how the Church raises money, or at least some churches, those that have graduated out of the raffle and jumble sale league.

To understand it we must go back to the New Testament and rid ourselves of confusing thoughts about stewards being cloth-capped union officials or barmen on oceangoing liners. In New Testament times every well-to-do landowner would have a steward. He would have been a senior slave, reasonably educated, competent and entrusted with considerable responsibility. He would have the care of all his master's possessions, including the other slaves, and would be personally accountable to the master for everything he did. He would have to be totally trustworthy for he had great power. But he had nothing which he could call his own.

Now perhaps you can see why stewardship, in this New Testament sense, is such a good description of the Christian's responsibility for everything that has been entrusted to his care. We own nothing, but we care for an enormous amount of God's property. 'This is how one should regard us,' wrote Paul, 'as servants [literally, slaves] of Christ and stewards of the mysteries of God.' And he goes on almost unnecessarily, 'It is required of stewards that they be found trustworthy' (1 Corinthians 4:1f). That goes without saying.

But what have you got to look after? Not much, you may say. Here's a list. Your body, which you inhabit, with its feelings, its thoughts, its powers and your inner personality that makes the real you. Your belongings, your money, your earning capacity. Your skills and aptitudes, your time and the way you make use of it (or not, as the case may be). Your world, which is God's world in which he has placed you. All this makes up the realm of your stewardship.

(a) *Your body*. While we all like to dream that we are perfect physical specimens, most of us are not. We have our limitations, our handicaps, our blemishes. We try to hide them but we know they are there. We have to live with the body we have been given. The body has its appetites and desires, and it is the seat of all our feelings and emotions. It has its own private world deep within where the mind operates, often quite independently of the body, as we know only too well when we dream or daydream.

All this is ours to do with as we want. We can starve it, we can indulge it; we can adorn it, we can destroy it; we can despise it, we can revel in it; we can neglect it, we can control it. Being a Christian adds a further dimension. Paul wrote: 'Do you not know that your body is a temple of the Holy Spirit within you, which you have from God? You are not your own; you were bought with a price. So glorify God in your body' (1 Corinthians 6:19f). That is to say, God dwells in your body by his Spirit, so that is an added reason why his dwelling-place should be well cared for and congenial for him to live in.

Your body can take a fair amount of punishment and hard wear. It is astonishingly resilient. It has a built-in self-healing and renewing mechanism, to which food and sleep contribute a good deal. At the same time it has a delicacy and refinement about its constitution which deserves to be respected. The more you study human anatomy the more awesome you find it to be. 'We are fearfully and wonderfully made', was how the Psalmist put it. This then is the complex and sophisticated human body which God has created for you to inhabit in company with him. What kind of caretaker are you going to be?

Well, obviously you must not misuse it. You owe it to God to keep it in good trim and as serviceable as it will ever need to be. You are not to experiment with it or deliberately to damage it. I can see no justification whatsoever for pumping it with tobacco smoke and nicotine, with excessive alcohol or with drugs that are not necessary for its healing and restoration. Over-eating too is just as harmful as over-drinking and there are some doctors who would regard obesity as one of the diseases of middle age which needs to be tackled no less ruthlessly than some of the more obvious illnesses.

But let's be positive too. Keep that body of yours healthy, well-groomed, exercised, properly rested and able to function to the peak of its capacity when called upon to do so. Don't ever let it master you, for it is yours to master and control in the service of your Lord.

(b) *Your feelings*. Because you are a human being and not an animal, you have a remarkably extensive range of emotions which well up within you. Anger, jealousy, pleasure, excitement, boredom, enthusiasm, hunger, self-pity – the list is endless and I don't need to go on about it. They are triggered off by obvious and predictable things such as insults or achievements or food or occurrences, some happy and some sad. They can also be set off quite accidentally or unexpectedly, as if by some unseen trip-wire, and the feelings burst in upon you before you have been able to identify what it was that set them off.

They all have a physical explanation, though pure chemistry does not tell you why they happen one day and not another, and certainly not in sufficient time to enable you to know how to handle them. It is your skill in handling your emotions which will largely dictate how you get on in life, whether you enjoy it or are made miserable by it, whether you sink or whether you swim. So your emotional life inevitably looms large in any discussion of Christian living and it is right we talk about it here.

It would be too simplistic to say that you either control your emotions or allow your emotions to control you. Remember that they are part of your human make-up and God has given them to you as indicators to help you make well-rounded decisions and to enable you to understand the inner workings of other men and women. The person who has blocked off his own emotional springs is pretty awful at handling other people. He simply no longer has the equipment to do so. But to say that your emotions are God-given does not mean that you always give them free rein. It could make you a very difficult person to live with. You may enjoy having your tantrums (small children seem to!) or wallowing in self-pity or living on cloud nine (for a few hours), but there is usually a price to pay and we none of us live on desert islands. The most important lesson to learn (and few people actually learn it) is that your feelings are your property and you can do with them what you will. You do not *have* to feel hurt by that person's snubbing you, you do not *have* to let yourself be so carried away by your recent success that you can never come safely back to earth, you do not *have* to be infatuated by that married man who has just smiled at you. Your emotions are yours for you to order and control, so you cannot get away with saying 'I couldn't *help* feeling hurt, angry, flaming mad, and so forth'. Of course you could.

I am not saying this is easy. I am just saying it is possible. It is something everyone has to learn, and the Christian has to learn it more than others. Because just as his emotions belong to him, so he remembers that he belongs to God. His feelings will be restrained by his obedience to God, for they have great potential for producing both good and evil.

Jesus spoke about this in the Sermon on the Mount, you may remember. Whereas Jewish law set boundaries to what people did: no murder, no adultery, no stealing, our Lord set controls on people's emotions that gave rise to those sins. So a certain kind of anger was tantamount to murder because it could lead there, and the lustful look was not very different from full-blown adultery because it was a basically sinful motivation which was common to them both.

The New Testament gives plenty of advice about our feelings, those which need to be encouraged and those which need to be restrained. The passage in Galatians 5:19–23 lists several of them under the heading 'the works of the flesh' and 'the fruit of the Spirit'. But while some emotions are good and others are sinful, there are many feelings which are morally neutral. Anger, for instance. There is a righteous anger which drives us to crusade for a better deal for the oppressed, and there is an intemperate anger which can lead to violence or worse. Paul said, 'Be angry but do not sin; do not let the sun go down on your anger, and give no opportunity to the devil' (Ephesians 4:26f). Quite clearly it was possible to have a non-sinful anger, but in his mind an anger which was allowed to fester overnight turned into bitterness or resentment which were fundamentally sinful. It is up to us to exercise the proper restraint and to make up the quarrel with the person to whom our anger is directed – before we go to bed.

Possibly the most difficult emotions of all to control are our sexual feelings. They have to be strong or the human race would die out! It does no good to ignore them and you certainly cannot eliminate them. They are a sign of healthy humanity and are, like the rest of your emotional make-up, a gift from God. But they can cause endless damage and destruction if they are not properly controlled. Letting go sexually, for which another word is being dissolute, or permissiveness, leaves a trail of unhappiness in its wake and it can never be pleasing to God or for that matter give you any lasting sexual satisfaction. So you have to keep your desires on a tight rein and do all you can to lead a pure life as a good steward of the gift of masculinity or femininity that God has given you. And if the struggle seems hard and endless, remember that you have the grace and help of God to call upon and his understanding, fatherly care to support you.

(c) *Your time.* Time is a very precious commodity, and the older you get the more you value it and the more you realize how much gets wasted. The high-powered businessman can have his time valued at hundreds of pounds an hour. You wonder how he can afford to take time off to eat his meals! But for all of us time has to be 'redeemed', which is the biblical word for it, so that it can be used to the best advantage. You see, time too is a gift from God and needs to be husbanded accordingly.

From the very earliest times God has taken an

interest in our time. That is why he taught his people to keep one day in seven 'holy unto the Lord'. It was to be a day of rest, of freedom from work, and a day dedicated to God. The Sabbath was a gift, not a burden, a time when God could be worshipped without the clutter of the workaday world troubling them. The Christian Sunday has inherited many of the blessings of this one day in seven, as well as being the great day to celebrate and commemorate Christ's resurrection. But the very fact that it is still part of the Christian routine (in the right sense) witnesses to the place that the proper apportionment of time has in the purposes of God.

As with the week, so with the day. The first call on our day is the time we spend consciously alone with God. If that time is well-chosen and kept sacrosanct, a sense of discipline will permeate the whole day. Most of the day will be given over to what we have to do – our work, our commitments in the home, eating and sleeping. Some time each week certainly needs to be given over to 'good works', i.e. acts of kindness done voluntarily to help other people. This would include voluntary social service, visiting the sick or the elderly, running errands, helping in a Brownie Pack or sweeping that wretched confetti away from the church porch (you see, I can't get it out of my mind after all these years!).

(d) *Your skills*. Most people are good at something, and some people are good at several things. Perhaps it is a natural gift, like friendliness or a love of music, or it may be one you have acquired by hard work, like playing an instrument or carpentry or micro-electronics. I am not going to say much about this, but aptitudes, whether natural or hard-earned, are a trust from God and so from time to time you will want to ask yourself, 'Am I using my talents wisely and well? Are others benefiting or are they wrapped and packaged just for my own benefit? Does my Lord regard me as a good and faithful steward of the gifts he has entrusted to me?' These are all questions that need to be asked and answered honestly.

(e) *Your belongings*. Chief among these will be the money you have and your ability to earn it. Again the Bible gives us a precedent. The old standard that was set was that every member of the community automatically gave one tenth of all his income to God and then made his voluntary offerings on top of that. Now the texture of society is very different today and incomes are reduced by taxation and other charges over which we have little control. But many Christians still try to live by a principle of tithing (giving a tenth of) all their income and they find it an extremely rewarding way of stewarding their belongings for God.

To start with, the best thing to do is to decide before God on what the proportion of your giving is to be, and whether you calculate it on your gross income or your take-home pay. Much will depend on your other commitments and so forth, so there is no hard and fast law that has to be obeyed. God only asks you to be responsible about it. It is not difficult to do unless of course you have already over-reached yourself on your commitments, which probably suggests you are living beyond your means anyway. It has always seemed to me that it is no harder to live on 90 per cent of your income than on 100 per cent, as long as you begin like that. Otherwise it will mean some gradual cutting back until you can afford to live on what is left over after God has been given his portion.

Once this kind of decision has been taken, the money set aside for God has only to be apportioned. Perhaps you have put it into a separate bank account, or a sock under the mattress, but you will need to decide how much of it goes towards your local church (at least half of it, I would think) and how much goes to other good causes, charitable, missionary and relief funds. Christian giving needs to be reviewed regularly, and constantly updated, but it is my experience that once it is dealt with in this orderly way your giving becomes a joy and your support for Christian causes and your response to appeals for help have the wince taken out of them, and it becomes a real pleasure to contribute to God's work and his children's needs. There are fringe benefits too, one of which is that you appreciate far more the other things you possess, almost as if the setting aside of a proportion of your money has sanctified the rest. You also learn to be economical, because you have to be, and you have a great sense of being rewarded by God because you are taking your stewardship seriously. It is a funny thing but many people who give like this will say that since they began tithing there has never been any real shortage of money to live on. I cannot understand the mathematics of this and I am sure it should never be the reason why you take up tithing, but that's what people say and I pass it on to you for what it's worth.

(f) *Your world*, which is of course God's world. It is one of the more enlightened features of modern life that we are becoming so much more environment-conscious. Mind you, it's high time we were, because for generations we have abused the world we live in, polluting its rivers, exploiting its mineral resources without a thought for future generations, poisoning the earth's atmosphere and putting commercial benefit before the good of the people who live here. We still have a very long way to go, whether it is in preventing the destruction of the ozone layer, cutting down on the acid rain or coping with the mammoth quantities of nuclear and chemical waste that are being disposed of in the earth – to say nothing of the technological junk that is hurtling around in space.

To my mind it is a little sad that it has often been humanists and not Christians who have been in the forefront of the 'green' environmentalist movements that are now influencing so many nations. For Christians have a special duty to subdue the earth and replenish it, in the words of Genesis 1, and this great passage teaches us that man is the caretaker of God's creation and is held accountable before God for the way in which he looks after it. What is called for is a sensitivity to the environment and a greater respect for its beauty and for the creatures which inhabit it. This becomes increasingly important as the earth's population increases, as forests are cut down to provide for man's requirements, as the seas are overfished and the fossil fuels are steadily used up without any possibility of replacement. At some stage people need to say 'Stop'. We have gone far enough. This earth is God's earth and not ours. We are his stewards and we have to hand it on to succeeding generations for them to enjoy.

We have ranged far and wide, from the feelings that are deep within us to the fuels that are deep within the earth, but both are signs and symbols of God's varied (literally multi-coloured) grace which we referred to in the opening sentence of this chapter, and of this grace we are to be good stewards.

Living it Out

As we come to our last chapter I want to take as my theme 'Work out your own salvation with fear and trembling; for God is at work in you, both to will and to work for his good pleasure' (Philippians 2:12f). You will probably have got the message by now that there is a world of difference between becoming a Christian and being a Christian, or to put it slightly differently, between being a Christian and living like a Christian.

Make no mistake, becoming a Christian and turning to Christ is the most important thing you could have done. By doing that you *are* a Christian. Despite your many sins, God has forgiven you; despite your continuing imperfections, God has accepted you. You belong to him and he has taken responsibility for you. He loves you, respects you as a person and wants you to *become* what you *are*. Your status as a Christian needs to develop into the character of a Christian. You have to live it out.

It will not happen automatically or accidentally. It demands effort, determination and a readiness for self-discipline. Those are the basic ingredients of the repentance which began you on this journey. But it is not all one-sided. True, you have to make the effort, you have to be willing to change, but at the same time the God who took up his residence in your heart when you came to him will by his Spirit change you inwardly, so that you want to be different and you also find you have it in you to be different. That is what our theme-text means when it says that God is at work in you, both to will (i. e. make you willing) and to work (i. e. make you capable) for his good pleasure.

The quality which God is looking to see develop in your life is *holiness*. 'Be holy, for I am holy' is the constant cry of the Bible from the early books of the Old Testament to the closing chapters of the New. But what is holiness? I am afraid we have not made it into a very attractive quality. It is associated in people's minds with solemnity, a slightly forbidding otherworldliness, and a set of people and things that are a shade divorced from the reality of the present world. But the real image of holiness is not like that. It does mean total dedication to God but with the warm, joyful, loving character that you associate with the Lord Jesus and with saintly people like Mother Teresa, if you don't mind me bracketing them together. And there is such a thing as 'earthy holiness' which can be attained even by bank clerks and working mothers and ordinary people like you and me. But if you don't like the word, leave it on one side and concentrate on being just 'Christian'.

Living as a Christian will work itself out in different ways in different settings – at home, at work, in your private life, in your social contacts. We can't be exhaustive here but let us take these four areas of life one by one.

(a) *At home*. Whether we are now living in our parents' home or in digs or have set up our own home, we all began life under authority as children in the home of our parents. They set the rules and as it was their home, they were entitled to. The home was meant to provide us with protection, security, a loving context and a place where we would learn and develop to maturity. No parents are perfect and children are even less perfect, so I have no doubt that you can look back on your early life as a child with a considerable sense of failure. You were not all that marvellous. But, cheer up: it may not be too late to improve things!

There are two lessons that can best be learnt at home, and if they are not learnt there they are either never learnt or learnt at much greater cost in later life. The first is how to be obedient and the second is how to apologize. Being obedient is necessary at home. Parents have a natural authority and the child has to learn to do as he is told. Parents have obligations too, of course, but that is not really your concern. You have the priceless opportunity at home of learning how to knuckle under and be obedient, even when you believe your parents are being unjust, simply because the person who cannot obey cannot be trusted with other people's obedience. When I was in the Royal Air Force training to be an officer, it was constantly dinned into us that we could never lead until we had learnt to follow. 'If you are ordered to jump into a lake, you jump into the lake. You can ask why afterwards', was the way they put it. Now, parents rarely ask for such unquestioning obedience but because they are our parents and see things we don't see, they sometimes ask us to do things we would never choose to do and cannot always see the sense in doing. But obedience says yes, and it is a good lesson to learn. It was said of Jesus that 'he learned obedience through what he suffered' (Hebrews 5:8), for he too had to submit to the will of his heavenly Father whose perspective was so very much wider than his human eyes could see.

Then, learning to apologize. This is one of the hardest things to do, especially to do it handsomely and not grudgingly (which is scarcely worth doing at all). It needs great character to say that you are sorry and to ask for someone's forgiveness. Small-minded people hide away and sulk, or else they go on insisting that they were right all along and they are never going to climb down. You never lose anything by coming down off your high horse. People think more highly of you than before and it will do you no harm at all. But home is where you can learn to do it, and where you can also learn how to receive an apology graciously without rubbing the other person's face in the ground.

The Lord's Prayer has quite a bit in it about forgiving and being forgiven, because God knows that both in our spiritual life (where we are sinners needing to repent and be forgiven) and in our human relationships (where none of us is perfect) we shall never go very far without learning this essential art of saying sorry and discovering the satisfaction of having a broken relationship mended. And we start to learn it at home.

(b) *At work*. I cannot be specific because for you work will mean anything from a classroom to a kitchen sink, but there are a number of principles of holy living which apply to almost every situation. I would put at the top of the list honesty. The Letter of James contains plenty of good practical wisdom, especially about how to tame the tongue, which it calls 'a restless evil, full of deadly poison' (James 3:8). It goes on to say 'Let your yes be yes and your no be no', by which I don't think it means be frank and forthright, but be transparently honest in what you say and do. Truth is sacred and needs to be held in high honour, so any touch of deception, half-truth or falsehood is patently wrong and an insult to the truth. The old saying goes that you have to have a good memory if you are going to be a good liar, but it is not good enough to be truthful just because you are very likely to be found out. The untruthful person is a faulted person, like a rock with a crack in it, and the whole of your character leaks out through the lies you tell. If people cannot believe you, what prospect have you of gaining any of their trust? Before you come back at me and argue about the legitimacy of the 'white lie', which is usually typified by not telling someone their mother is dying when you know she is, let me say that there is a world of difference between softening the truth for the sake of some greater good or a person's greater need and concealing or distorting truth for selfish or deceitful ends. If, when the truth comes out, the person can thank you for keeping some of it back, the sacredness of the truth has not suffered and your integrity has not been lost. So don't lose it: it is a most desirable quality to have.

Next to honesty comes the old-fashioned virtue of diligence. This is enshrined in the Old Testament proverb: 'Whatever your hand finds to do, do it with your might', or in my grandmother's dictum: 'If a job's worth doing, it's worth doing well.' I am not quite sure if this attitude of mind is included in the so-called Victorian work-ethic, which it is fashionable to look down upon these days (for some reason I don't fully understand), but it sounds like good Christian commonsense to me. For the Epistles urge me to do my work 'as to the Lord and not to men' and 'not in the way of eye-service, as men-pleasers, but as servants of Christ' (Ephesians 6:6f). Clearly nothing but the best is good enough for God, so the best it must always be. Apart from anything else this approach to my daily work gives it a dignity that would otherwise be lacking. To skimp a job, when you could do it better, to spin it out, when you could do it in half the time, to give what you know not to be value for money, is guaranteed to debase the value of work and to destroy the sense of pride that work done in God's name and for his sake should generate. So, whether it's homework or housework, benchwork or deskwork, do it with all your might and you will not go far wrong.

(c) *Your private world.* There is a whole world at work beneath the surface of our public lives which is the private world of our thoughts. No one else has an inkling of what goes on down there and most of the time we are very thankful that they don't. Only occasionally does it show through an expression on our face or an inadvertent word, but otherwise it only finds expression if we choose to make it known – and even then we will present it only in the way we want it to be seen or heard, not necessarily how it really is.

There is no reason at all why God should be excluded from this world and indeed he has a right to be there. In fact he *is* there, for nothing can be hidden from him though we may not want to acknowledge his presence. Adam and Eve were not the only people to hide away from God when they felt ashamed of themselves.

Our thoughts need the purifying light of Christ if they are to be kept from the darkness and chaos that can so easily dominate that hidden world. We have already mentioned how prayer is a way of letting God into those inner recesses and we come back to the same point now. For though we call it our private world it is not private at all. Our thought-life eventually influences the visible part of our lives, for better or for worse, so we can well understand why Paul, for instance, wrote about taking 'every thought captive to obey Christ' or urged his readers that 'whatever is true, whatever is honourable, whatever is just, whatever is pure, whatever is lovely, whatever is gracious, if there is any excellence, if there is anything worthy of praise, think about these things' (Philippians 4:8). As the old saying goes: 'A man is

not what he thinks he is; but what he thinks, he is.'
Or, as I was taught in my boyhood: 'Sow a thought,
reap an action; sow an action, reap a habit; sow a
habit, reap a character; sow a character, reap a des-
tiny.' It all begins in the mind. So let Christ reign
there in your private world.

(d) *Your social life*. We come finally to the world
of your relationships with other people, your leisure
activities, your sports and pastimes, your holidays,
your social life at church, your relationships with the
opposite sex. All in a couple of pages! Once again
we must confine ourselves to the basic principles,
and the bottom line is this: 'You shall love your
neighbour as yourself.'

Your neighbour is everyone with whom you have
any kind of relationship. And to love him is to
respect him as a person, made in the image of God
and of value to God. To love is to be sensitive to
his feelings and to try to see life through his eyes.
It does not mean to be affectionate towards everyone you meet. Some you will like instinctively, some
you will not like instinctively. You cannot help that.
It is how the human chemistry works. Obeying our
Lord's command to love is a different matter altoge-
ther from liking or feeling friendly.

The model that he gave us is that of the good
Samaritan. The religion of the day said that you
were to love your friends and hate your enemies.
Samaritans were enemies with whom you avoided
contact as far as possible. They were renegade Jews,
outside the covenant. But in Jesus' parable it was
the Samaritan who broke the mould and helped the

Jewish stranger lying in the road, so that in future it was possible to love both your friends and your enemies. They were still outside the covenant, but they were people and they deserved to be treated as such. The test of whether we keep God's commandment to love our neighbour as ourself is how we treat people we do not get on well with, the outcasts and strangers of our lives. It is basically a matter of respect.

Respect is also basic to our relationships with the opposite sex. If we fall for the popular advertisement lie that women are just sex symbols, we shall treat them as such if we are male, or behave as such if we are female. There is no respect or love in that. It is an adolescent fantasy unworthy of adult human beings and is poles apart from the teaching of Christ. The Bible's view on human sexuality can be summed up thus. God has made us male and female, and this is very good. Sex is a gift to be enjoyed within marriage and not outside it, or its good purpose is nullified or abused. Extra-marital sex is adultery and is forbidden: its destructive power is enormous. On the same reasoning pre-marital sex is out, because it has no commitment and is essentially selfish. Homosexual sex is unnatural and not a part of God's gift to the human race. The gift is too valuable to be used in a way that was not intended. Anything less cheapens it and degrades the person or persons involved.

So, go for the best. Stay pure and don't be conned into anything else. That is not the way to happiness nor is it the way of God. And if you live by this standard, your relationships will be enhanced rather than the reverse. People will know you can be trusted: you are not the sort to take advantage of them. And the respect you show will be shown to you in return.

Finally, I want to thank you for listening to me because I feel as if I have been speaking to you rather than writing a book. I am not sure if I have done any good. That will be for you to decide. For going on with Jesus is the way you have set yourself to follow and you must see it through.

But, remember. You are not alone. God the Father who made you is with you. God the Son, our Lord Jesus Christ, who died for you, is alive and is with you. God the Holy Spirit who has been given to the Church is within you. The three persons of the Holy Trinity are all on your side as you go on in the Christian life. You should manage. And my prayers will be with you too. God bless you.